Start Me Up!

Start Me Up!

Sonia Williams

First published by Exisle Publishing Ltd

www.exislepublishing.com

Published by Accent Press 2010

ISBN 9781907016509

Printed and bound in Malta

Cover design by Lyn Jones

Contents

Contents

Introduction

For some people, new and innovative ideas simply flow from their creative being. For others, coming up with a business concept is like trying to find the proverbial needle in a haystack. It can be incredibly frustrating. Deep down you yearn to own and operate your own business and you know you would make a great businessperson. The only barrier to your entry into the business world is coming up with the seed – the idea. However, just because you haven't had your own light-bulb moment that doesn't mean you shouldn't be in business. You may very well have all the necessary skills, experience, commitment and passion to run your own company successfully, and denying yourself that opportunity simply because you can't find the right starting point could end up being a lifelong regret. *Start Me Up!* is written especially for people who are searching for that starting point. I want you to exploit the ideas in this book; after all, sometimes all we need is a helping hand to get on the first rung of the ladder of success.

But before I introduce you to the contents of my book I would like to quickly introduce myself. I have worked as a qualified Certified Practising Accountant (CPA) in several large corporate enterprises as well as government-based organisations and small boutique accounting practices. Nominated for the prestigious Telstra Business Women's Awards in 2008 and 2009, I have also published three books, two of which are bestsellers in their category: *Show Mummy the Money* and *Give it a Go: what have you got to lose?* What makes me an expert in this field is the fact that I have been there and done it, both online and offline, and I have lived to tell the tale. I have personally established several businesses, from wedding photography to publishing to bookkeeping. I have continued to set up diverse businesses over the last ten years, and successfully grow these businesses, simply because I know how to seize a great business idea and act upon it. I have also made some of the fundamental mistakes that trip up many entrepreneurs along the road to riches, and I have discussed some of these in the course of this book, in the hope of preventing you from following in my footsteps!

Over time I have had many people ask me how I came up with the ideas for my various businesses. It isn't rocket science, but it does take an open mind and I soon realised that it was not something everyone could do. So I felt compelled to write this book, since there are so many people from all walks of life who could make very good business people if they only had the inspirational seed to kick-start their journey. This is the purpose of *Start Me Up!*: to provide budding entrepreneurs with the platform to maximise their entrepreneurial skills and make the most of opportunities before them.

The key to sourcing new and exciting business ideas is to open your mind and live life considering every experience to be an opportunity. If you have a negative experience with a product or service, don't get upset. Instead, consider whether this is fate calling. Could you turn the situation around and develop a business opportunity from your experience? There have been many entrepreneurs over the years who have successfully turned a bad experience into a multi-million-pound business opportunity.

The best part about living in a modern and ever-changing world is that nothing's perfect. There are limitless opportunities for entrepreneurs to get out there and improve the world we live in.

I often hear self-limiting statements such as 'I couldn't possibly start a business; I am not an entrepreneur'. One of the best things about being an entrepreneur is that there are no boundaries; there is no job description for 'entrepreneur'. You don't have to conform to certain criteria to become one. There are no age restrictions and it certainly doesn't matter what colour, creed, race or religion you are. Anyone and everyone has the opportunity to become a successful entrepreneur as it's more about visualisation and actualisation than anything else. When you can visualise what you want to achieve, you can start to see how to make it happen.

This book is about providing you with the motivation and inspiration to see how you can make something happen. It doesn't matter if you have just left university, are looking for a career change, are a stay-at-home mum or have partially retired from the workforce. The information in this book is designed to help you switch on the light-bulb moment that lies dormant within you. Over the course of this book I will explain:

_ how you can discover the business opportunities that already exist within you

2

_ how you can capitalise on the latest trends
_ and, most importantly, what you need to consider before you bankroll any new idea.

And if that doesn't help you come up with an idea, I have done the hard work for you by detailing more than 100 fantastic business concepts!

Irrespective of the business opportunity you decide to capitalise on, the key to success is to pursue opportunities you are passionate about. But I don't mean passionate in terms of how much money you could potentially earn from the opportunity. Truly successful businesses are those founded by people who are passionate about what they do – 'the cause'. Consider the example of the The Body Shop, an international success story founded by mother of three, Anita Roddick. Anita not only had the savvy to tap into the body beautiful market, she succeeded because she was unequivocally passionate and committed to social and environmental change. Success does not normally flow from ventures where the main objective is purely to make money. Seek out a market you desperately want to work in. Find a product or service that really interests you. To be successful in business you need to live and breathe the merits of your product or service.

Second, you also need to do your research. You can have the best idea at your fingertips, but without proper market research, a business plan and a crystal clear understanding of who represents your target market, you could very well turn a good idea into a great disaster. Information is power. With research you can better mould your idea and work out how to effectively launch it to generate maximise exposure. More importantly, proper research will help you to ensure your idea will be a money-spinner.

I cannot stress this point enough; sadly too many excited entrepreneurs set up businesses in a fit of exhilaration and fail to do their homework. Don't become one of the statistics; take the time and effort to conduct research. It won't necessarily prevent you from making mistakes altogether but it will certainly limit their severity. In Chapter Four I set out exactly what research you need to do.

Finally, here's one more bit of advice from a seasoned entrepreneur: along your journey to becoming an entrepreneur you will experience many highs and lows. When enjoying the highs, take the time to smell the roses, and when you dive down into what can seem like the depths of despair, remember there is only one way from here and that's up. To claim that the journey of a small-business owner is easy is a mistake of massive proportions. It's not. However, the freedom to work when you want and how you want, to be in charge of your own financial future, is exhilarating to say the least. To balance the scales you have to expect to hit a few brick walls before you are able to finally smash through and experience success. The road does indeed get easier as you take more and more steps along it – this is the benefit of experience. But you will only gain that experience if you actually opt to take the path well worn by many successful entrepreneurs before you.

Good luck on the roller-coaster ride to becoming an entrepreneur!

The idea is

right under

your nose

The search for the optimal business opportunity can be distracting. We get caught up in an endless search and forget to look at ourselves and assess our key strengths. What is your field of expertise? Do you have key strengths or some professional experience you could capitalise on?

In this chapter I will help you to think about exactly what sort of business you could be running by detailing how to:

1. assess the 'YOU' business opportunity
2. draw on life experiences
3. put the cart before the horse
4. identify a niche market.

Ask yourself what you are good at. What are your core skills and strengths? Do you have any particular skills or professional expertise that could be utilised for the development of a business? Write them down.

Don't just answer 'no'. Everyone is good at something.

The trick lies in recognising how you could

turn this into a profitable business opportunity. For example, are you good at dispensing advice? Do friends and family continually seek your opinion? Perhaps you could capitalise on this skill by becoming a counsellor and charging for your advice. Do you regularly receive a mountain of compliments on your competence in the kitchen? Why not consider starting a catering business or running cooking classes to impart your superior cooking prowess? Maybe you could write a cookbook with your own secret recipes.

If you have a hobby you could capitalise on it. Alternatively, if you have a keen interest in a particular subject you could consider taking your interest one step further by turning your interest into your business. For some budding entrepreneurs their love of the environment has been the catalyst for their start-up ventures.

Leveraging off your skill set, interests and hobbies is a great way to start a business. If you start a business in an unfamiliar field you will undoubtedly face a steep learning curve. However, if you already have an intimate knowledge of and interest in your chosen field you will find it much easier. If you have memberships in various organisations, associations or clubs related to your hobby or area of expertise, you will find you already possess vital contacts that you can tap into to help establish the business.

Whether your family is your hobby or whether your interests lie elsewhere, it is important to recognise those interests that could make a new venture work, and work well. When I started my photography business I had a genuine love of weddings, a passion for photography and a talent for working with Photoshop®. In fact, I was addicted to weddings and took great pleasure in capturing this special day for other couples. But because I did not have professional experience in the field of photography I did find it harder to establish the business. Ideally, when assessing yourself, consider what you do best and work to your strengths.

Take Mike and Clare Brown, a man and wife team from Wiltshire, who created the D'ARCY BROWN brand in 2003, following long corporate careers at the Walt Disney Company. On the birth of their first child, they found it wasn't easy to buy stylish, but practical clothing not covered in logos, or seen on every other child. They set out to design clothes; classic, but not traditional; clothing that still makes children look like children. In June 2002 they bought Kent & Carey, a shop in Fulham, with a 10-year history in making classic clothes. They quickly realised it wasn't viable just to make clothes for one shop. So D'ARCY BROWN, the brand, named after the couple's newborn daughter, was born. After UK success, with 200 independent retail clients, and department stores including Fortnum & Mason, Harrods, Fenwick and Hoopers, the passionate and driven couple set their sights on cracking lucrative international markets. With "Market Entry Support" from UK Trade and Investment (UKTI), they were encouraged to visit the clothing exhibition 'Children's Club' in New York. Since first exhibiting there in Spring 2007, orders have been flooding in. They have deals with 40 online and long-established stores. As US exports go from strength to strength, D'ARCY BROWN has also started exporting to Ireland, again with great success as this market also discovers the unique styling of this brand. Now that's not bad for someone who started off just trying to meet their own children's needs! www.darcybrown.co.uk

Turning a hobby into a flourishing business is not just for those with a flair for craft. Nick, Charlie and Matthew Otley are the founders of one of Wales's largest independent craft brewing companies, Otley Brewing Company. For the three brothers, their beer enterprise started out back in 2005 as a determined attempt to break the mould of real-ale thinking and banish the well-worn image of "the woolly cardigan and beard syndrome". The Brewery originated when they had the idea of producing award-winning beers the likes of which had not been done in Wales before. As a micro-brewery, they are dedicated to the craft of producing Welsh ale with a difference. Using the highest quality ingredients with every effort made to source produce from the local area, including fresh Breconshire water, the finest malts from Newton Abbot and fragrant hops from Malvern.

They had the idea to launch a brand that would appear fresh, modern, simple and a little intriguing. The 'O' prefix for their broad range of beers comes from their surname Otley. They have compiled a range of simple names based on this: O1, O2, OBB, OG, O8 and even a Dark O stout.

This was simply a way of labelling the products almost like an industrial stamp rather than a flowery meaningless name. It was to prove popular with the new young drinking scene, a sector of the market not normally associated with real ales. Suddenly they had products visually not putting up barriers to new drinkers, young people and women who were key to their products' success. They have just launched a new website, www.realbeerbox.com, branded in the same style as the brewery and hope to grow the brand further in the future. www.otleybrewing.co.uk

2. Draw on life experiences

Sometimes coming up with a successful business concept may be a matter of reviewing your own life experiences. Have there been any situations where you thought: 'If only the product or service did ...', 'If only the product or service was ...', 'I wish there was a ...'? These sorts of situations are seeds. This is exactly how some successful entrepreneurs have come up with fantastic, innovative, award-winning ideas. Their products or services were born out of necessity. If you spend a little time thinking about your own personal experiences and how 'it would have been great if there had been ...', you will soon find a variety of business concepts come to mind.

This is exactly how engineer Dr Keith Alexander came up with the Springfree™ Trampoline, the 'world's safest trampoline'. Dr Alexander was motivated to come up with a safer trampoline for his own children to use after his wife refused to allow them to use the dangerous old-style one. After fourteen years and millions in research and testing, he delivered the perfect product, revolutionising the way consumers perceive traditional trampolines.

According to Springfree™, over 150,000 children worldwide are admitted to hospital each year after suffering injury on the springs and frame of old-style trampolines, or by falling off. Dr Alexander sought to design and create a recreational trampoline that was significantly safer and more fun to use. He succeeded. I know – I own one myself. It is the very first trampoline without coiled steel springs and is designed to remove all the traditional impact areas that cause equipment-induced trampoline injuries. The trampoline hit the market in 2003 and is now sold in fifteen countries with new sales regions coming on stream each year. It is distributed exclusively in the UK by Rainbow Play Systems & Costco UK.

Further testament to its success is its inclusion as a finalist in various prestigious International Design Awards, which recognise superior design and innovation.

www.springfreetrampoline.co.uk

Judith and Clive Freane are an inspiration to suppliers of local organic produce. In the early 1990s they took over the family farm that had a long-established herd of Guernsey dairy cows. Recognising the growing trend towards organic foods and keen to preserve both the breed of cows, which was becoming more rare, and the local Somerset habitat, they decided to turn the venture into an organic one. At the same time, their beef produce was becoming increasingly recognised for its superior taste. Taking a leaf out of home-delivery enterprises such as door-step milk already well-known in the UK, they set up Brown Cow Organics to supply their own growing market. The dairy produce arm of the business took a further leap when they began to produce organic yoghurts for River Cottage, in association with TV chef Hugh Fearnley-Whittingstall. They have since diversified into old-fashioned varieties of vegetables grown for their flavour rather than yield. The concept has proven a winner, with many consumers happy to by-pass the larger and often foreign-owned distribution chains to buy direct, or via Farmers' Markets. Since 2001 they have received a host of food, organics and other accolades, including the Triodos Bank "Women in Ethical Business" Awards for 2007 and 2008. They have also been recognised by more of the UK's top chefs such as Rick Stein and Jamie Oliver. **www.browncoworganics.co.uk**

Sue Ismiel emigrated to Australia in her teenage years. By her early thirties, Sue had married and was the mother of three daughters. As a result of the need to find a depilatory cream for sensitive skin for one of her children, Sue created a natural, revolutionary hair-removal gel in her own kitchen. Experimenting with items from her pantry, Sue invented a 'green goo-like substance', which she named Nad's. Nad's was unique; it contained no chemicals and did not require heat for its application, unlike traditional waxes. With no scientific background and no business skills or experience, Sue invested £3,000 of her long-service leave and started selling Nad's at local markets, and then on television via infomercials. Both the domestic and international retail market has sought out Nad's. In less than a decade, Sue Ismiel has created a multi-million-dollar business, with Nad's Natural Hair Removal Gels, Strips and Wands becoming one of the leading brands worldwide, for women and increasingly for men, too.

Her business success has been recognised by numerous awards including Ethnic Businesswoman of the Year (1999); induction into the Businesswomen's Hall of Fame (2000); the 2002 Ernst & Young Entrepreneur of the Year (Retail, Consumer and Industrial Products); Sydney *Business Bulletin*'s Business Star of the Year; and *Sydney Business Review* Businesswoman of the Year. As recently as 2009, in the September edition of *Pure Beauty* magazine, Nad's was credited with Best Hair Removal Launch Awards for their Hypoallergenic Fragrance Free Facial Strips and their Natural Warm Wax. www.nads.co.uk

While vacuuming his home, James Dyson realised his bag vacuum cleaner was constantly losing suction power. Dust would quickly clog the pores of the bag and block the airflow, which resulted in a rapid drop in suction. So James, an industrial designer by training, decided to solve the problem and invent a bagless vacuum cleaner. It took more than five years and 5127 prototypes to perfect his design, but in the early eighties James introduced to the world the first cyclonic bagless vacuum cleaner.

James Dyson offered his invention to major manufacturers. One by one they turned him down, apparently not interested in new technology. They seemed determined to continue selling bags, a lucrative market. Today James's persistence and patience has paid off. By 2005 his vacuum cleaners had become popular in both Europe and the United States, with the rest of the world soon following suit. In 2008 it was reported his company's revenues had reached a staggering $1 billion. In James's own words: 'You know the feeling when some everyday product lets you down. "I could have designed this better myself," you think. But how many of us turn our thoughts into actions?' www.dyson.com

3. Put the cart before the horse

Consumers are grouped into various target markets categorised by their unmet needs, and these target markets are made up of many different social groups, such as pensioners, new home buyers, parents, singles, teens, children, babies, same-sex couples, the fashion-conscious, gardeners or DIY home renovators. (These groups are just the tip of a *Titanic*-sized iceberg.) An alternative method for identifying a great business idea is to start by deciding on which target market you could serve and what its unmet needs are. Essentially you are working backwards. By identifying the needs of the consumer first, you can then undertake your own brainstorming session to uncover ways to satisfy those needs successfully.

Let's consider an example. With advances in medical technology and healthier lifestyles, we can now look forward to a longer life expectancy. So who is catering for the needs of the ageing population, the baby boomers? This target market provides a golden opportunity for the budding entrepreneur. Start by considering what the unmet needs are. For one segment of the ageing baby boomer market, retirement represents travel – both international and domestic. In the past five years there has been a sharp increase in the number of caravans purchased. With this in mind, what products or services would help these customers achieve their travel ambitions, given their age and physical condition? Could you offer a specialised travel service – Contiki tours for seniors? What products would make travelling easier?

For other boomers retirement is about living life as comfortably as possible. Business opportunities exist in designing the necessary equipment, utensils and accessories to help the elderly achieve this ideal. For example, better designed cookware for people with arthritic hands or recipe books adapted for those with poor eyesight. Services required by this segment of consumers could include running errands, shopping, or helping with cooking and other domestic chores.

You can see from this example how by identifying the target market first you can then start to consider what unmet needs exist, and how you could successfully satisfy those needs. Remember, a great idea need not be ground breaking or earth shattering, it simply has to satisfy a particular group's unsatisfied needs.

4. Identify a niche market

Gordon Gekko introduced the saying 'Greed is good'. But in business, greed is not good. Many budding entrepreneurs fail to see the benefits of servicing a niche market. Rather, they prefer to target a broader market in order to maximise sales. The fact is that it is far more profitable and cost-effective to target one segment, a niche market, within a much bigger market. If you try to cater to the needs of a total market you may well miss out on an opportunity to satisfy the needs of a smaller subgroup successfully. Using the example above, ageing boomers interested in travel form a target market with specific needs. However, the niche within this market might be those who seek to travel overseas or those who prefer to travel the local countryside in a caravan. Breaking the overall market down into attractive niche markets is often the key to a successful business.

This is exactly what Donna Hubbard, founder of Gymophobics, has done. Seven years ago, Donna identified and pursued a niche market within the total health and fitness industry. The idea was to provide a health and fitness centre for women with issues with their figure that catered not only to their health aspirations but also to self-esteem needs. Hubbard has said "If you are like so many women that I meet who want to improve their figure and fitness but hate the thought of going to a Gym, then Gymophobics is the place for you". Her club is a women-only club, not just a fitness centre, for women who want to feel good about themselves. Not only did Donna find a niche ready to be served, she opened at the right time. The fitness boom is well-known, health awareness has been given a big push by media outlets and baby boomers continue to be aware that growing old gracefully isn't going to happen during an extended lunch with a bottle of chardonnay. People are ready to act. Women want a place of their own and Hubbard is there to serve their interests. Gymophobics now operates 32 gyms, with another 8 opening shortly What Donna did right was recognise a niche market and create a product that suited the needs of this market perfectly. Take a moment to think about what might happen if you find the right target market before the kids leave home. The possibilities are endless. And like Hubbard you might even be able to begin a multi-million-pound trend. Donna has her imitators, but Gymophobics are growing to be one of the strongest of the women-only gyms. Why? The reason is simple. Finding the right niche target market and the product to service that market before anyone else means that it becomes very difficult for your competitors to surpass you, particularly if you continue to innovate. www.gymophobics.co.uk

Serial entrepreneur and founder of the premium job site Six Figures, Kelly Magowan is another excellent example of how you can benefit from segmenting your overall market to identify and target a niche market from within. Six Figures is a leading job site for businesses who want to recruit from the top level of job seekers, offering employers access to professionals on more than $100,000 a year. Instead of appealing to any and every job seeker and employer, Magowan established a business that effectively assists in the matching process, bringing together the top 10 per cent of jobs with the top 10 per cent of job seekers across all industries and professions, permanent, contract and part-time. Because Magowan targeted one specific market within the overall recruitment industry, Six Figures was able to create a solid reputation and a strong brand identity that is known for matching highly talented individuals to top employers. Within 6 months of its launch in 2008, the company went global and is now linked with executive recruitment worldwide! Check out www.executivesontheweb.com

By now I hope you can see that, irrespective of the business concept, you will create greater leverage and strength by targeting a specific niche market with unmet needs.

To help you to realise the type of business you should be involved in, complete the following activities.

The objective is to help you identify where your interests, strengths and key skills lie.

Activities to help you identify which business is right

Exercise 1

1. What are you interested in? What are you passionate about? (This can include causes, such as water conservation, environmental or social interests.)

2. What are your hobbies? What do you enjoy doing in your spare time?

3. What are your key strengths? What do you do best? (Perhaps you are a fantastic cook; maybe you have a great ability to write or draw; or you might have specialist skills developed from your professional career.)

Exercise 2

1. Briefly describe a situation where you thought 'If only there was a ...' , 'Wouldn't it be great if someone ...?'

2. Now write down how you would do things better? How could you improve the situation?

Exercise 3

1. Reflect on what you have just written. Is there an idea there? How could you capitalise on these strengths or interests in the form of a business?

Capitalise

on the

trend

Changing world trends are just the place to start your search for the elusive next big thing! Trends are driven by a range of factors, including pop culture, media, news, innovation and the arts. However, more often than not, changing and evolving consumer needs dictate and underline world trends. To be successful in business you need to be aware of what is going on in the world around you. What are the hot buttons that will have consumers eagerly opening their purses and wallets to make a purchase? Underlying the success of many businesses is the identification of changing world trends.

Trendsetters are successful entrepreneurs because they set a pattern of behaviour that is readily emulated but rarely surpassed. A good place to start when considering setting up a business is to examine the trends that have influenced you. Once you have done this, take a look at a few major trends and see if you can determine why they were successful. If you can predict where future trends are heading you can effectively identify ideas that are worth pursuing.

It is important, however, to be able to distinguish between a trend and a fad. Anything that has staying power can be classified as a trend. A trend evolves and develops gradually, following a sequence of events that allows you to trace it back to its origins. Trends do not start out with immediate acceptance; it is only after a period of time that they become mainstream. Trends tend to have a social, political or economic influence. Fads are here today, gone tomorrow; they don't tend to become mainstream – a bit like a one-hit-wonder song. You can still capitalise on a fad if you're smart enough to get in and out before the fad has passed, but your success will be very much dependent on timing.

Spotting trends takes research; you need to be observant and alert to changes in popular culture. Read newspapers and magazines, especially those from popular and fashionable cities as these are where trends are often born. Go online, read blogs, watch TV, especially the news and popular shows – what topics are they canvassing, what are their similarities, what are the main themes? Look at large corporate companies and research where they are spending their product- and market-research budget. Do all that you can to stay on top of what's hot and what's not…and what will be in the future.

You don't need to do a lot of deep thinking to figure out what's a good idea or trend; a simple Google News Search based on topics of interest and potential trends will produce results you can analyse. Not all the results returned by the search will be relevant, but this helps demonstrate whether a trend is a no-brainer.

Let's examine some hot trends and potential business ideas that could well lead you to the next big thing. I have provided some great examples of businesses from around the world that are already successfully riding these money-making trends. Quite a few are from Australia – a market with many close parallels with the UK, which I have particular knowledge of. I hope you can glean some inspiration from them and come up with a slightly different idea of your own.

Trend 1: Customisation and appealing to individual needs

Some years ago businesses competed by producing goods and services en masse. Products and services were simply commodities. But as time passed, more and more businesses produced the same uniform commodities so business owners found they needed another way to differentiate their products and services. The nineties produced a dramatic change: the marketing gurus started to run the show. Powerful marketing strategies tapped in to the consumer's psyche, emotionally trapping the customer. There is no better example of this than the marketing strategies that have successfully got teenagers to spend £150 on a pair of trainers made in China for probably 10 per cent of what they sell for.

The New Age consumer has arrived. The era of 'individual marketing' and the need for customisation has dawned. We simply know too much. We have unprecedented access to information. As a result we have become far savvier consumers. In the coming years more and more consumers will prefer to purchase products and services that cater to their individual needs. To remain competitive, businesses will need to focus on these needs, customising products and services accordingly. Mass production of identical products and services will be replaced by the flexible production of customised products.

The consumer's desire for customisation has enormous implications. It is predicted that many consumers will, if they haven't already done so, turn 'anti-brand'. This emerging trend will see many large well-branded companies ducking for cover. Their challenge will be to find new ways to build customer relationships and provide genuine individual customer service. But due to their size and scale, these larger businesses will find it difficult to create the personalised touches and experiences desired by the New Age consumers. Smaller businesses have a greater opportunity to personally engage their customers by better understanding the consumers' needs and developing products and services accordingly – offering excellent opportunities for the savvy entrepreneur in the process.

To make the most of this emerging trend, consider the many products and services people consume on a daily basis. How many of these do customers wish were more tailored to their specific individual needs? Now consider whether there is a smaller group within the overall group that you could successfully satisfy. Have you got a subset of individuals in mind? Voilà! You are on the road to a great business idea.

All types of products and services can be customised. Clothing can be made to order; food can be specially prepared to suit individual palates; children's toys can be made on demand, customised to the child's favourite colours and branded with their name. This trend favours small business owners: they can readily tailor production and manufacturing of products or services because, unlike larger businesses, they don't produce in large volumes. The devotees of custom-made are also willing to pay for individuality so small business owners who customise to suit the needs of their target market have a real opportunity to charge, with justification, premium prices.

Some examples of industries and products that lend themselves to customisation are:

_ fragrances
_ cosmetics
_ skincare creams
_ clothing
_ cards and gift wrapping
_ hand-crafted personal diaries
_ photo albums.

Let's look at some examples of innovative businesses that have achieved great success catering to the individual needs of consumers.

Me and Goji retail made-to-order breakfast cereal online. They provide their customers with the opportunity to mix and match up to 70 different ingredients to create their very own unique breakfast cereal. www.meandgoji.com

Evlove Intimates makes 'made to order' intimate lingerie. Evlove offers customers the opportunity to create personalised lingerie products through a direct-selling distribution model. Customers design their own lingerie by selecting from a number of designs, samples, fabrics, appliqués and accessories. www.evloveintimates.com

Aussie Murals produce bold and exciting wallpaper feature walls, panels, canvases and photographic murals. They provide a custom service, allowing their customers to tap into their own creative juices. You can choose a design and custom colour it to suit your taste or existing décor, or you can personalise your mural or canvas by sending them a photo or your favourite artwork or an individual design. www.aussiemurals.com.au

MyShape is an online retail store where women can find clothing matched to their measurements and body shape. The founders of MyShape were inspired by a common problem shared by women of all ages and sizes: 'finding clothes that both fit well and flatter the various body shapes'. www.myshape.com

You can see from the examples above that the owners of these businesses have in each case identified a viable niche of consumers who desired an end product customised to their specific requirements. They have then provided their target market with that opportunity to customise.

Trend 2: Go green

Protecting the environment and better managing the world's limited resources is a growing industry. There is a wave of concern and realisation that the consumption of certain goods and services is having a negative impact on the environment. We are already seeing signs of this developing into an industry with a number of new products and services designed to help protect and better manage our environment. In fact, many large corporations have already seen the economic and environmental sense of going green. Recently, media mogul Rupert Murdoch of News Corp launched a major initiative aimed at bringing the company's carbon emissions footprint down to zero by 2010. News Corp plans to achieve this significant reduction by:

_ providing incentives for Fox Entertainment employees to buy hybrid vehicles
_ placing energy-efficient products at various media outlets like the New York Post
_ investing in green-friendly initiatives such as a wind farm in India to offset carbon emissions.

You can bet that when the likes of News Corp start to implement environmentally friendly practices and activities the industry for sustainable products and services is set to take off.

Society will continue to move away from activities that harm the planet. The recent shift from the use of plastic bags at the supermarket to calico and paper bags is a clear example of how consumer behaviour is changing, reflecting a greater concern for the protection of our planet and an awareness of the need to become environmentally friendly.

The state of our environment provides a number of opportunities for the budding entrepreneur – when environmentalism meets business you get enviro-preneurship! Individuals and businesses will come to depend upon technologies, products and services to provide for the long-term sustainability of our natural environment. With a little creative thinking there is a fantastic opportunity to create products and services designed to effectively replace what is currently available and satisfy the world's need for sustainability. In years to come more and more consumers will base purchasing decisions on the positive or negative impact their purchases have on the wellbeing of the environment. Recognising we live in a world of finite natural resources, consumers will be forced to do their part. Out of necessity, sustainability will become the norm.

Areas where new and innovative products and services will emerge include:

_ biodegradable products and services
_ alternative means of producing energy, e.g. solar energy
_ recycling programs
_ reducing pollution such as carbon emissions
_ reducing water consumption
_ education programs for business and individuals – how to manage our finite resources better.

The flip side to recycling is 'heirloom products'. Instead of purchasing recyclable products that are used for a relatively short time before disposal, consumers are starting to look for long-lasting, iconic products that can be passed on to following generations. There are opportunities for future businesses to find ways to adapt timeless quality to high-tech gadgets. The development of improved, high-quality, longer-lasting products will also create new trading sites. We will probably see a boom in luxury second-hand and vintage stores, both online and off.

So how can you go green and take advantage of this growing trend? Do a bit of research; start to look into what will be the major environmental challenges ahead. Then examine how you can play a role in successfully overcoming these challenges with a modern business solution. Now this is not to suggest you need to be a superhero; you don't need to locate millions of pounds to build a laboratory with the aim of discovering the solution to global warming! It's all about looking at the environmental issues on a relatively small scale. Take, for example, the innovative mums who came up with the simple and effective concept of designer shopping bags. Janina Byrne and Celina Jorgensen are the founders of www.envirotrend.com.au , a concept they came up with over a bottle of champagne in 2006. They spotted a gap in the market: while being environmentally conscious is important to both women, neither was keen on toting around ordinary green bags – especially outside the supermarket. These fashionistas took the typical green shopping bag and gave it a timely makeover; their designer shopping bags are made from 100 per cent recyclable non-woven polypropylene. Such was the success of this simple and effective idea that their first shipment of the initial product, the EnviroShopper™, a stylish alternative to supermarket green bags, sold out in just three months.

So you can see you don't necessarily have to come up with a groundbreaking solution to the world's environmental problems. Instead, just think what you can do that is in line with the growing trend towards environmentalism. To help get your creative juices flowing, let's look at some more creative business concepts from around the world. These are innovative businesses that are making a living from helping to protect the environment and relieve the demand on our scarce resources.

Todae have a great a range of ecologically sustainable products and services to help consumers and business owners maintain and develop a more environmentally friendly lifestyle. Instead of inventing new environmental products and services, Todae conveniently grouped a range of selected products and services in the one location, making it easier for the customer to choose and use environmentally friendly products. As well as household consumables (such as cleaning and body care products), there are energy- and water-saving devices for the home and office such as shower timers, low-energy lighting, biodegradable pens and recycled printing paper – all designed to help consumers reduce environmental damage. They also offer practical advice on how to cut down energy and water use and to offset the carbon emissions from your car, home or from air travel. www.todae.com.au

Ecolimo also spotted an excellent business concept that was in line with the growing going-green, environmental trend. Ecolimo offers Melbourne's first environmentally friendly limousine service using the hybrid Lexus GS 450h luxury sports sedan. They recognise more and more people will choose green technology to reduce their carbon footprint and accordingly have given the consumer a choice. www.ecolimo.com.au

Realising that a growing number of consumers are opting for

non-chemical-based cleaning products, the founder of Cinderella Bex Gold designed ecologically sound home-cleaning products. Cinderella products are 100 per cent safe for the environment, replacing the need for petroleum distillates, ammonia or phosphates to clean the home. The ingredients of the Cinderella product range contain plant-based surfactants from renewable resources that are nine times more biodegradable than standard surfactants. www.cinderella.com.au

Trend 3: Time is money

Time is the new currency. More and more people are searching for ways, products and services to give them back quality time – from the humble microwave that speeds up cooking time to GPS devices that take us where we want to go without the need to waste time checking a traditional road map.

Here is your opportunity to make a little money by giving back to the consumer his or her 'time'. What service or product could you produce that saves time or gives back time to the consumer? There are many daily activities that we all undertake which consume our time, but what if you could eliminate one of these activities? Let's consider quickly the UK-based property site www.rightmove.co.uk . Since 2000 this site has meant homebuyers no longer need to go from one estate agent to another looking for properties. Co-founders Ed Williams, Miles Shipside and Nick McKittrick literally brought the homes for sale to the buyer's fingertips, not only saving prospective buyers precious time but also allowing them the luxury of viewing potential properties all from the comfort of their own home.

There is no doubt that over the past decade our lifestyles have become increasingly hectic and chaotic – we are busier than ever. Consumers will continue to source ways and means to save time. In our parents' era, hiring a cleaner was unheard of unless you were filthy rich. Nowadays you don't have to be rich, simply time-poor. It is quite the norm to pay someone to do your 'dirty work'. Eating out or ordering in is no longer considered a luxury; it's a necessity for many people. First it was takeaway and home-delivery outlets that caught on to this trend. Then the Internet became an important tool, not only for diners but shoppers as well. With precious little time available, why bother getting into the car to go to the shops, fighting for a car space then dealing with the hustle and bustle of other shoppers, all for a loaf of bread? Using the Internet to make routine purchases and have them delivered is fast, convenient and easy. This evolving trend continues to provide opportunities for the budding entrepreneur. When you work hard and play hard there is little time left to scrub the toilet. So what can you do to save time for a select group of consumers? There is an endless list of tasks that could be outsourced, from walking the dog and gardening to cleaning the house or doing that most evil of things, the ironing. If you can find a way to make the life of a modern career-focused, overworked, extremely busy individual easier, then that consumer will reward you handsomely – after all, time is money.

Many women are returning to pursue careers with a family in tow, creating opportunities for the budding entrepreneur to come up with creative ways to save these mums time.

Look at your own daily routine. What are the activities that consume a great deal of your time over the course of a day? Could these be outsourced?

Some areas where time could be saved include:

_ household errands
_ the care of elderly parents
_ housework and home maintenance.

Think about all the time-consuming activities that today's time-poor consumer will undertake in their lifetime: buying a car, purchasing a house, arranging a wedding, choosing electronic equipment, preparing the house for the arrival of a baby, locating the right school – the list goes on. These are all areas where the smart entrepreneur can step in, satisfy a need and make a little money. Let's take a look at some successful time-saving concepts that have been transformed into operational businesses.

DoMyStuff.com is an online community where busy people can quickly find assistants to complete their chores. Errands can range from the mundane, such as mowing the lawn or picking up dry cleaning, to the extraordinary, such as arranging dinner with a celebrity or chartering a private jet. Individuals can post an errand on DoMyStuff.com and potential assistants or businesses located within the vicinity compete by bidding to complete the errand. This bidding system ensures that the user finds the best person to undertake the errand at the lowest price, saving the user valuable time. www.domystuff.com

Pop to the Shops offers customers the opportunity to shop with local independent retailers and producers for products and produce that aren't available in nationwide stores. Customers of Pop to the Shops can shop at any time for local products, from the local butcher to the greengrocer, all in one purchase. Pop to the Shops saves consumers valuable time: they no longer need to rush around trying to fit in with the shorter opening hours of smaller independent local businesses. Since delivery is free, Pop to the Shops generates revenue by charging retailers 10 to 15 per cent commission. Pop to the Shops has also ensured it is not confined to one specific area by designing its systems to enable territories to be created for certain postcodes and co-ordinated by a single person. www.poptotheshops.net

A study by food giant Parmalat has found village shopping is all the rage. For example, up to 80 per cent of Australians shop at least once a week in their local 'village economy', and local shopping centres are believed to be influencing choices of location for housing, reports the Australian Financial Review. Monash University's Michael Morrison says individuals may fulfil their cravings for community connections by visiting nearby, family-run shops. Parmalat's findings suggest the 'pop to the shops' trend could probably work in any well-developed economy populated with time-poor consumers.

Flylite is helping frequent flyers avoid the hassles of waiting at baggage carousels, having their suitcases searched by security staff and dealing with lost luggage. The company provides an inclusive service, picking up and delivering a member's bag as well as packing the bag and dry cleaning the contents. Finally Flylite keeps the contents in storage until the customer's next flight. Flylite supplies the suitcases, which the customer packs with the clothing they would typically take on a regular flight. For example, for someone in business this might include a suit, shoes, toiletries and so on. The packed case is returned to Flylite where the contents are inventoried and placed online. The customer can browse through their wardrobe and select what they'll need for their next trip. Flylite saves their customers time, enabling them to simply breeze in and out of an airport, luggage-free, to find their suitcases waiting for them at their destination. www.flylite.com

MyTickets is a website designed to help the user find tickets faster. It's similar to a search engine except that it's exclusively for tickets. Instead of hunting through multiple websites and making numerous phone calls, the consumer can use MyTickets as their one-stop destination to find the tickets they want. The site includes listings from all major ticketing websites, event websites, and even lots of the less well-known websites that are harder to find. www.mytickets.co.uk

Trend 4: Blooming baby boomers

A baby boomer is someone born between 1946 and 1964. The 2006 revision of *World Population Prospects* by the UN Department of Economic and Social Affairs Population Division predicts the number of people 60 years of age and older will nearly triple to 2 billion by 2050, accounting for nearly a quarter of the expected 9.2 billion global population. This is a huge target market and presents an excellent opportunity for the budding entrepreneur.

Ageing, for some relatively well-off populations, is creating opportunities for products and services aimed at making older consumers' lives easier. According to Mary Furlong, author of *Turning Silver into Gold: How to profit in the new boomer marketplace*, there are market opportunities in medical devices, such as those designed to combat or assist with deterioration in hearing or sight. Mary also says opportunities exist for large-screen computers; mobile phones with larger numbers; good-quality designer hearing aids that look more like jewellery than a hearing device; menopausal nightwear; and technology to enhance cognitive fitness or improve health and wellbeing, such as devices to monitor sugar levels for the growing number of pre-type two diabetics. She predicts that by 2020 there will be 120 million people with mobility problems – a huge market.

It is important to note, when assessing the opportunity offered by the baby boomer market, that you have to set aside any preconceived notions about the profile of a baby boomer. The stereotype is evolving. The psyche, education and experience of those individuals approaching 50-plus is changing. Many understand the Internet and are technologically savvy, and they all know what they want.

Areas of interest or concern to baby boomers, where a potential business idea may arise, include:

_ financial management – reducing bills and expenses
_ health issues – dealing with hearing or visual impairment, loss of mobility or arthritis

25

_ housing – downsizing or renovating the family home
_ the empty nest – early loss of a partner or children moving out of home creating new singles
_ technology – baby boomers may need help installing the latest gadgets, electronic equipment, etc.

Baby boomers have worked hard and now they expect to enjoy life – but not in a nursing home! Perhaps a retirement village where the elderly are treated with care and respect and which is run more like Club Med than a hospital might be a winning idea. There have been several innovations over the last ten years that have been designed for an ageing population or adapted especially for them, particularly in the area of skincare. Feeling a little thin-skinned? Try Botox! But what else does this market need?

To identity the business opportunities surrounding this target market of consumers, perhaps you might like to spend a day or two with your own grandparents or offer to help out at your local community centre where the elderly may convene for a particular class. If you want to see what the market does then get in amongst it.

For now, let me show you some brilliant business concepts from around the globe that specifically cater for the needs of this generation.

Jitterbug has come out with a cell phone especially designed for baby boomers and their parents who find trendy cell phones too complicated and small. Great Call Inc.'s Jitterbug Dial phone features a traditional dial tone to show the phone is ready to work, a padded ear cushion to improve the caller's ability to hear, large fonts on an oversized keypad and a 'phone concierge' where you can enter and delete numbers in the phone's directory. The company says, 'The phone has the appearance and size of a typical flip phone.' It was developed by Great Call President Arlene Harris, 58, and her husband, Chairman Marty Cooper, 78, who invented Motorola's first cell phone in the 1970s. www.jitterbug.com

A growing number of employment agencies and recruiters cater for the mature worker. With the world taking a great financial hit recently, many more retirees are coming out of retirement to compensate for their financial loss. There is also a growing recognition from employers that they must look outside traditional age ranges to find the expertise they need. The US Federal Bureau of Labor Statistics says the number of workers 55 years and older who are employed has been growing. In 2006 employment in this age group increased 5.6 per cent in the United States – more than twice the rise in the overall employment level. For some it's about the need to make ends meet, for others it's simply about wanting to keep busy. Human resources experts from RetirementJobs.com observe that a long-predicted workforce change is now under way – possibly the biggest change since women went to work en masse in the 1970s. www.retirementjobs.com

The founders of Readerwear recognised that baby boomers were not satisfied with the selection of reading glasses stocked in local chemists. Subsequently, they established Canada's first specialty retailer of ready-to-wear reading glasses. The founders say they realised 'people wanted more choice and more style, without having to pay a couple of hundred pounds for prescription glasses'. They offer over 700 different styles of ready-to-wear reading glasses in diopters from +0.75 to +4.00. www.readerwear.com

Jeff Taylor launched www.eons.com in 2006. To date it is the largest website launched that specifically targets the 50-plus market. According to the award-winning online publication for small business owners, Small Business Trends, the site's traffic recently topped 500,000 unique visitors per month. Eons provides members with the tools for social networking and user-generated content, including message boards, online self-assessment tools, and content-ranking and voting systems. Eons hosts over 1000 discussion groups, many of them user-based.

House Works focuses on the provision of personal care assistance, companionship, home modification, cleaning and relocation services. House Works is dedicated to helping seniors live independently, no matter how challenging their circumstances. Focusing on a customer driven approach, House Works returns a sense of control to adult children and their elderly parents. www.house-works.com

Driving Miss Daisy is a cab service specifically for senior citizens. Like its movie namesake, it provides transportation to take customers shopping, to doctor's appointments and social events. Driving Miss Daisy prides itself on providing extra care and security for its elderly customers at affordable prices, something more than the service provided by the average taxi driver. Transport services should work particularly well if marketed not only to senior customers but also to their busy children, who don't always have enough time to help their parents as much as they would like. www.drivingmissdaisy.net

Trend 5: Health, fitness and self-improvement

The wellbeing revolution continues to gain momentum, having experienced positive growth over the past ten years. Increased awareness of the benefits of a healthy lifestyle has promoted the growth of a number of alternative practices, such as holistic healing through natural remedies and products like essential oils and herbs. This trend will continue to grow. Not only have we become a self-obsessed society in terms of the food we eat, but we are also very conscious of how we look and how we feel. The consumers who support this trend can be categorised into a number of smaller segments. There are those who seek divine intervention to deliver the body they believe will make them 'bootylicous'. Others simply want to maintain their fitness for the purpose of achieving longevity. A further group suffers from various conditions such as obesity or diabetes – a market desperately seeking a healthier lifestyle.

You can certainly profit from this trend but you do need to think outside the square. After all, let's face it, 30 years ago if we were told there would be money to be made in selling bottled water because it's supposed to be better for you, we all would have laughed. Sadly bottled water today costs more than a litre of fuel – who's laughing now? So you can see there is plenty of money to be made by helping consumers reach their peak level of wellbeing.

Maybe you could consider starting a business in any one of the following areas of opportunity in the health, fitness or self-improvement industries:

_ alternative therapies
_ stress management, relaxation and meditation
_ personal counselling and self-awareness
_ parenting skills and techniques
_ public speaking and social etiquette
_ career and skills development
_ image consulting
_ personal security and self-defence training
_ personal-fitness training

_ diet and nutrition
_ adventure sports.

However, to be really successful, you need to add a twist to your offering. Consider, for example, personal development classes aimed at teenage girls. They could be a cross between a finishing school, image consultancy and life-counselling service – helping young teenage girls make the transition into young, confident, assured women.

The health industry is a large market still worthy of exploration. Healthcare, food services, and the manufacture and sale of medical devices all have something to offer consumers who want to lose weight. Parents are encouraged to motivate their kids to join in athletic activities. You might like to consider a business focused on physical exercise for kids. This is an emerging market and with a little fine-tuning you could stand out from the businesses that already exist in this area. Take the idea one step further and you have 'gyms for kids'. No need to build Arnold Schwarzenegger-style bodies, but some light weight training and a workout routine could be the basis for a lucrative business. Locate the business inside a larger gym and run your sessions while mum and dad are de-stressing on the treadmill.

Are you stuck for inspiration? Never fear, here are a couple of ideas from around the world that I hope will get you thinking about the best business concept to fulfil your entrepreneurial ambitions. The following are great examples of businesses following this trend while also offering a unique point of differentiation.

With rising concerns about childhood obesity, a profitable market to tap into is likely to be that of health- and weight-conscious parents. Generation Now Fitness was established by Jane Silber as a result of helping her nine-year-old daughter deal with a weight problem. Jane found most gyms didn't allow children to come in and work out, and those that let children in didn't have the right-size equipment for them. Subsequently Jane opened Generation Now Fitness for tweens and teens, equipped with state-of-the-art interactive fitness facilities dedicated to obtaining and maintaining the physical and mental wellbeing of children, including kid-size, fun-to-operate exercise equipment, a smoothie bar, a study room and other amenities. www. generationnowfitness.com

VocationVacations provides customers with the opportunity to test-drive their dream job, empowering their clients to turn their passions into a career. VocationVacations has tapped into a serious dilemma faced by many – which career path should I follow? This is a daunting prospect particularly for young adults. Few people can truly say they are doing what they love, but it doesn't have to be like that.

VocationVacations enables people to experience one-to-three-day, hands-on, dream-job-immersion experiences under the tutelage of expert mentors – try before you buy. It's like test-driving a car, except here you're test-driving your dream job. www.vocationvacations.com

Bus Bike is a mobile gym, fully equipped with sixteen indoor bikes and an instructor, as well as a dressing room, fridge and sound system. Passengers pay a monthly fee for two to three classes a week. To avoid problems like traffic jams, the bus is fitted with a GPS system. Similar to a typical public transportation system, the business has fixed pick-up points, departing at set times (on the hour), and operates Monday to Friday. www.busbike.com.br/i_index.htm

Nuun manufacture electrolyte replacement tablets. The tablets are designed to create a hydrating drink for sports enthusiasts once added to ordinary water. Nuun was developed as a result of the frustration experienced by the founders in their search for a lightweight, easily dissolvable electrolyte hydration solution that was free of carbohydrates and could be used in remote places. Nuun is pioneering portable electrolyte hydration for athletes and those with active lifestyles. It's easy to store the tube in your pocket or pack then just drop a Nuun tab in your water bottle when you're running, cycling, hiking, adventure racing, kayaking, golfing or travelling. www.nuun.com

You can see that the breadth of this trend is enormous; you can literally come up with dozens of ideas for related businesses. Health and fitness, whether mental, emotional or physical, will always be of great concern for most people. You already have a target market; all you need to do is work out what you can offer to help these people achieve a higher level of health and fitness.

Trend 6: Food glorious food

Food is the topic on everyone's lips – how much or how little we eat, what we are eating and where. We are constantly bombarded by the media, who exacerbate our obsession with food by publicising the latest, most successful diet or exposing large corporations who use a number of potentially unsavoury ingredients to create their products. Serving to further fuel this trend, there is now a greater awareness of the link between healthy living, wellbeing and what we eat. *The Biggest Loser* has encouraged a significant change in the menus offered by the large fast-food companies. McDonald's has adapted its menus to include salads. Schools are carefully reviewing what is on offer at the canteen. There seems to be a new wonder diet endorsed by health experts every week. Many different and varied ideas can emerge from this trend.

Clothing
Individuals who are larger in size have a number of different needs and clothing is one of them. Sadly, we can all see the increase in the number of kids who need modern 'plus size' clothing, but how many designer brands actually cater for larger children in their clothing sizes?

Fear of food
A growing new phenomenon, 'food fanaticism' – the fear that food can kill – is affecting how some consumers differentiate between competing products. Supporting this trend is the explosion in food allergies and the identification of certain ingredients that either exacerbate or benefit conditions like ADHD or asthma. A number of food manufacturers have already recognised the value in this by producing foods laced with the very latest scientific know-how and technology. We now have butters and margarines designed to reduce heart attacks and lower cholesterol levels, milk with added calcium to strengthen the bones, and food to fight depression. It's no wonder that organic produce – perceived to be healthier – is starting to gain mainstream acceptance.

Micro foodies
Over time we will see an increase in micro food producers. Micro in this context means smaller businesses catering to a select number of consumers, as opposed to large national manufacturers producing for the masses. Examples include micro-breweries, micro-cheese-makers, gourmet supermarkets and boutique eateries. You can

apply this evolving trend to just about any category of food, even down to the most routine everyday food items like pet food.

Eating on the go

Where and when we are eating is changing. Nowadays life is so frenetic we often eat on the run. We spend less and less time actually preparing food, let alone sitting down to enjoy it. The business opportunity in this trend lies in focusing on developing authentic and convenient products that combine our need to be healthier with other needs such as portability and ease of preparation – healthy food on the go! In the good old days this was also known as fruit.

So what sort of business ideas can come from this trend? Well the sky's the limit really. Tap into a niche market and you could find you not only have your cake but can eat it too! For now let's digest some inspiration from across the world.

Dessert-only restaurants, such as ChikaLicious, have taken off in the United States. These 'dessert bar' restaurants cater to a unique niche market in retail food by serving only desserts – not your typical chocolate mudcake but desserts like those served in fine-dining restaurants. There are also themed desserts, from curry-scented concoctions named 'Voyage to India' to fanciful meringue creations. The founders have tapped into a niche market for sweet tooths who want to have their cake and eat it but not pay for an entire meal. www.chikalicious.com

Meal preparation is undergoing an overhaul through the provision of an innovative service – dinner assembly stores. Companies like Let's Dish! offer a meal assembly service for time-starved consumers, especially working mums. It's an innovative and convenient way to provide families with nutritious, tasty, home-cooked meals. Meal assembly stores focus on eliminating the hassle of meal planning and preparation by facilitating cooking sessions in a professional kitchen where customers can assemble twelve to 24 healthy family meals. Once prepared the meals are taken home to be consumed or frozen. This service saves the consumer valuable time by eliminating the need for grocery shopping, chopping and dicing, and cleaning up. www.letsdish.com

What our kids are eating at school has become a hot topic of late, partially fuelled by the attention given to the subject by celebrity chef Jamie Oliver. The basic mantra is to get junk food out and bring whole foods in. Lunch4Kids is the business idea of two entrepreneurial mums. Packaged like a McDonald's Happy Meal, each lunchbox contains sandwiches, milk or juice, a piece of fruit and a snack such as yoghurt, a cookie or a baby cucumber. Parents can order online, nominating the specific foods their youngsters would prefer to eat. The lunchboxes are delivered to participating schools every morning and invoices are sent directly to parents. The system keeps things simple for schools – no administration, no refrigeration. Besides the obvious advantages of balanced meals and healthy variety, there's also a high convenience aspect to Lunch4Kids. Parents don't have to worry about what to pack or panic if they've run out of fresh bread or juice boxes. According to parents who participated in the trial run, this alleviates morning stress and makes breakfast a time to enjoy with their families. www.lunch4kids.com

Take the concept of food and combine it with the growing demand for homemade and authentic products and you have a business like Foodzie. Foodzie is a US online marketplace where you can discover and buy food directly from small-scale, passionate food producers and growers. Their mission is to help change the way people eat while helping small food producers across the country find customers and grow their business. Foodzie claims: 'We're a bit obsessed with good food and passionate about connecting those that like to eat it with the people that make it.' www.foodzie.com

Trend 7: Handmade

Not to be confused with customisation, handmade is about keeping it real. Handmade products are unique, as the fact that they are not produced by machine means no two products can ever be the same. This trend is growing in popularity as consumers seek out greater individuality in their purchases. They want their purchases to make them feel special – part of an elite club far removed from the 'Joneses'. Globalised mass production simply does not offer the consumer the opportunity to say, 'It's a one-off ', whereas handmade does.

This trend is driven by the needs of the more mature and experienced consumer who seeks authenticity, style, artisan quality and uniqueness in the purchases they make. So how can you profit from this trend? Take a closer look at everyday products. What products could be handmade? The answer is just about anything, from children's toys and clothing to household goods. Here are a few examples of businesses handmaking their fortune.

Etsy is bringing together buyers and sellers of all things handmade. Best of all, Etsy provides a window onto a world market for the budding 'craft' entrepreneur. Since its launch in 2005, this online marketplace for handmade goods has grown to include tens of thousands of sellers across the world. To open up your own store on Etsy, simply register on their home page. I suggest you consult the FAQ and read up on the terms and conditions before you sign up. To ensure authenticity there are restrictions on what is deemed handmade. www.etsy.com

Madeit is an Australian version of Etsy. Since this independent directory of Australian designers launched late in 2006 it has evolved into a comprehensive directory, with over 130 independent designers listed…and growing. Madeit takes the frustration out of finding new talent on the Internet. The directory also provides the designers with a means of selling and distributing their wares. Selling is restricted to Australian residents only, however buyers from overseas are welcomed. www.madeit.com.au. To sell in the UK, you should also look at MyEhive, www.myehive.com

Chances are it would be difficult to replicate the success of Etsy and Madeit; however, this doesn't mean you couldn't take the same concept but specialise in one particular product or even sell your own wares on each of these sites.

From Paris catwalks to its stores in Sydney and Melbourne, G&L Handmade Shoes has become a secret shoe destination for celebrities, designers and stylists. Levon Karapetyan was only fifteen years old when he took a summer job in the factory of the renowned Armenian shoemaker Spartak. By seventeen he and his brother had started what would go on to become G&L (Gevorg and Levon) Shoes. Gevorg opened a factory in Armenia, while Levon moved to Australia to open a retail store in Sydney's Paddington and later Melbourne's Prahran. www.glbros.com

Marsha Hall Shoes is also another bespoke shoemaker based in Surrey specialising in creating the most exquisite handmade shoes or boots for any occasion, from day wear to weddings, or any other special event. www.marshahall.com

RedBubble is an online art gallery with a creative community providing users with an online marketplace and print-on-demand service to help them unleash their creativity. Through RedBubble you can:

_ display your creative work and raise your profile
_ connect with a vibrant community of creative people
_ turn your designs into physical saleable products like framed prints
_ offer your creative work for sale in a hassle-free way.

This site provides budding artists with a fantastic opportunity to display their work and break into the marketplace. You could well make a fortune selling your works of art to the world through RedBubble. www.redbubble.co.uk

Trend 8: Product recycling

There's a saying that one person's trash is another person's treasure. Today product recycling has taken on a whole new meaning. Budding entrepreneurs are turning trash into treasure and profiting along the way. They are creating everyday products with great designs that incorporate recycled materials into the production process. Since the items used are recycled, many products are limited editions. This is in line with the customisation and handmade trends previously discussed. Product recycling provides the budding entrepreneur with many business opportunities and is also a cost-effective means of sourcing raw materials that might otherwise cost a fortune from a wholesaler. Following this trend, a business owner can appeal to a variety of different target markets, from environmentalists to the hip and funky.

What products could be made from recycled materials? Is there another use for a worn tyre tread? Can plastic bottles be melted into another form? Can scrap paper be pulped and reincarnated as new paper? The opportunities are endless; all that is required to profit from this trend is a little imagination. So let's look at some innovative examples of product recycling and let's try to kick-start your own creativity.

Alchemy looks at its product design from an ecological point of view. By using materials that are normally discarded, such as tyre tubes and seatbelts, then adding a dash of imagination and plenty of hard work, Alchemy creates unique bags that are waterproof and whose durable rubber exterior won't easily stain. Best of all, they are made entirely from recycled materials. **www.alchemygoods.com**

Feuerwear creates bags and belts from used fire hoses. Designed by engineering graduate Martin Klüsener, the accessories come in red or white and are handmade. Since every product is fabricated from a different piece of fire hose, each one is unique. **www.feuerwear.de** (click on the English flag)

Another example of the product-recycling trend is demonstrated by Worn Again. This company has been giving a new lease of life to old materials such as car seatbelts, prison blankets, bicycle tyres, parachutes, firemen's uniforms and loads more. Essentially this business is responsible for 'up-cycling' pre- and post-consumer and corporate waste materials into stylish and relevant fashion products for a new consumer market. Working in collaboration with Virgin, Worn Again makes a unique range of bags using old Virgin Atlantic seat covers, thereby also helping Virgin Atlantic to meet its goal of halving the waste they send to landfill by 50 per cent by 2012. **www.wornagain.co.uk**

Freitag bags are handmade out of recycled truck tarpaulins, car seatbelts, bicycle inner tubes and used air bags. Designed in Zurich, the bags can be sourced in countries around the world. Freitag allows customers to design their own bag, through their interactive website. **www.freitag.ch**

Another great site to check out is Haul, **www.haul.com.au**. Haul recycles various materials into new funky accessories; for example, they rebirth used PVC advertising billboards into a range of versatile tough bags designed to carry anything you care to load into their spacious interior. Best of all, each one is an original. Haul also produces a range of products for a variety of enterprises using both found and recycled materials to create art pieces, furniture for bars and cafés and urban lifestyle accessories. At Haul a number plate can become a journal, a truck tyre inner tube a bag. Now Haul is a well-known street accessory brand. Also have a look at the UK-based site **www.shoprecycle.co.uk**

Consider what resources are wasted, then identify how you could use these wasted resources to make a product or service that a niche market of consumers would happily pay good money for, and, voilà, you have your business concept.

Trend 9: Indulge me please

Perhaps high levels of stress and the fast-paced lifestyles we lead have resulted in the self-indulgent trend of 'treating ourselves to life's little luxuries'. It seems people are more than willing to indulge themselves, for the most frivolous of reasons, regardless of whether they can actually afford it. But today's consumers are looking for something that offers a step up from the ordinary. It has been said that luxury will have a vastly different meaning for Generation Y than it does for Generation X. Those born in the '80s and later will opt to control their life. They will seek out what's fun and will be less likely to accept an executive job, since the hours are too long. They will probably be more concerned with experiences and less concerned with the accumulation of material possessions.

This is a fantastic trend to pursue and businesses catering to this new breed of fun seekers could find themselves well rewarded. There are many viable business ideas; it's simply a matter of identifying the 'right' indulgence. Consider a tea drinker for example. A special blend of tea leaves, spices or herbs could well be the product to give that consumer a well-deserved lift.

The key to harnessing this trend is to identify which products or services people will see as luxuries and be prepared to pay a premium for. Consider the following:

_ The number of beauty treatment spas that have opened over the past two years.

_ The number of premium hot chocolate cafés, where a hot choccie will cost you a whopping £3.

_ The rise of gourmet ice-cream parlours, where gelato is made from real fruit and costs twice as much as a commercial tub of ice-cream.

Note that for some consumers the trend of paying dearly to be pampered spills over to their pets as well. After all, they're part of the family too!

For some, indulgence is about more than material possessions. It's about experiences. We are about to enter into an experience economy, if we haven't already. We seek to indulge in experiences full of fun and adventure; we want something a little different from pamper ourselves and lift us out of the mundane. There are business opportunities to be seized by those who can identify the next divine self-indulgence or thrill.

Babymoon Guide offers expecting parents a pre-baby vacation, hence the term 'babymoon'. Many US travel and tourism agencies now offer babymoon weekends of pampering that include shopping trips for baby clothes and couples' massages. The 'World Travel Market Global Trends Report 2006' cited the babymoon as an illustration of the way in which travel and tourism companies are carving out increasingly customized packages to target different life stages. This new indulgent trend has significant appeal for expecting parents – the last hurrah of pure escape! www.babymoonguide.com

For an Australian version of the babymoon concept you need only look at the Palazzo Versace on Queensland's Gold Coast, which offers expectant mums a package called What's Kickin'.

www.daystoamaze.co.uk and www.adventure-events.co.uk both offer their customers an opportunity to indulge in an out-of-the-ordinary experience, from cooking lessons with a famous chef to hot-air balloon lessons to Ferrari drive days. But for a romantic experience look no further than Erin Kirkness, founder of Romantic Rooms, www.romanticrooms.com.au. Erin is responsible for providing couples with a sublime romantic experience. She has made it her business to create romance, from rose-petal-themed hotel rooms to guiding the nervous would-be groom through the process of a proposal, ensuring an experience both partners will happily recount to grandchildren. Erin currently operates out of Perth and Melbourne, with plans for other states as her business grows. Room for Romance, www.room forromance.com, is also worth tapping into for romantic hotels in the UK, Europe and Australia..

As you can see from the examples above, there's no limit to the products and services you could offer a society of self-indulgent consumers. All you need is a little imagination to work out how you can tickle the fancies of a defined target market.

Trend 10: The product or service makeover

At times it may seem difficult to come up with innovative ideas for products and services and quite often the costly nature of innovations limits the number of pioneering products or services introduced by the small business owner. However, all is not lost. With a little creative thinking some budding entrepreneurs have taken everyday products and services and added a modern-day twist to reignite and fuel consumer demand. We will all continue to need basic essentials – food to eat, soap to wash with, furniture for the home and clothes to wear – but what can you do to add your own contemporary twist that will appeal to the needs of a niche market?

In essence, this trend involves taking a well-established product or service meant for one market then tailoring it to satisfy the needs of a totally different market. For example, a niche market of pet owners serves organic beef and red-wine casserole fit for human consumption to their pets. Consider also the extensive range of skincare products now available to the male consumer. Skincare businesses have recognised they can take the concept of grooming, usually dominated by women, and apply it to men. This evolution of beauty therapy has even given rise to a new category of men – metrosexuals.

The most innovative business ideas often come from different contexts. For example, the iPod wasn't built from scratch; Apple simply took the characteristic style and simplicity of their computers into the music environment. Similarly one of the most popular worldwide travel sites, www.expedia.co.uk, took the typical travel agency experience online – no need for overheads and a string of offices, what a saving!

Making over a product or service is all about merging ideas from disparate contexts. The opportunities are limitless; all you need is a little creative ingenuity. For now let's look at some novel entrepreneurs who have thought outside the box and created a fresh new look for an age-old product. You may well find that by reading the following examples you discover a product or service of your own that's in need of a desperate makeover.

The Laundress provides a collection of high-end detergents for superior fabrics such as wool and cashmere as well as a special range of detergents and fabric conditioners for baby clothes. The founders researched and developed their own solutions to simplify and master the art of laundry. They took a tried and tested product used for generations and created an entirely new brand that recognises every fabric type is different and therefore, to ensure its longevity, should be treated differently. Who would have thought laundry detergent could become so technical? www.thelaundress.com

The takeaway industry is witnessing an upgrade of everyday takeaway food with the common burger and pizza undergoing a timely makeover. In recent times a number of gourmet takeaways have popped up, serving up everything from gluten-free pizza bases to 100 per cent organic beef and free-range eggs on burgers. Traditionally regarded as unhealthy, fast-food favourites are being converted into something that's still a fast favourite but which is made from fresh natural ingredients and repositioned as a nutritious alternative to a home-cooked meal. Proving that any product is worthy of an upgrade, these takeaway outlets are able to charge a premium price for their products. The host of awards and the recognition received by these outlets further endorses the power of this trend. To see some examples check out the fast-growing takeaway businesses www.grilled.com.au and www.easttakeaway.co.uk.

Even the secretive and sometimes tacky world of erotic adult products is undergoing an upgrade. Kiki De Montparnasse has taken what was once a sleazy industry and added elegance and class. This luxury fashion and lifestyle brand celebrates intimacy and inspires the romantic imagination. No cheap websites here; instead Kiki De Montparnasse appeals to a more sophisticated and stylish target market, offering a range of products from luxurious designer lingerie, jewellery and intimate accessories to bath, body and beauty products – all beautifully designed and elegantly packaged. www.kikidm.com

Everyday stationery has also undergone an extreme makeover. Kristina Karlsson is the founder of kikki.K, a chain of boutiques offering stylishly designed and fashionable stationery, home office products and accessories. kikki.K has revolutionised the world of stationery, particularly products designed to organise the home office and working environments better, by turning ordinary bland folders into colourful, contemporary and fashionable décor. www.kikki-k.com.au. In a similar way, Flujo have an impressive range of office furniture and accessories on their site. www.flujohome.com

You can see from the examples above that the budding entrepreneurs behind these business ideas have not reinvented the wheel to create their good fortune; they have simply re-energised a product or service to satisfy the changing and complex needs of today's consumers better. To ride the waves of success on this trend, take a look at your own world: what products or services could you improve on?

Trend 11: Piggybacking

Smart entrepreneurs accept that it would cost a fortune to try to compete with major players in a particular industry such as eBay, Google, Apple and so on. Instead they opt for considering creative and innovative ways to feed off the success of such large businesses. 'Piggybacking' on the success of a worldwide phenomenon is another trend that offers up great opportunities for the budding entrepreneur. For example, in the United States there are franchise stores piggybacking on the success of the world's first online flea market, eBay. eBay 'drop-off stores' have been established to collect and sell items belonging to those who don't have the time or know-how to do it themselves. iSold It opened its doors for business in December 2003 and has been going strong ever since. www.isoldit.com

In 2005 one stay-at-home mum piggybacked on the success of shoe phenomenon Crocs. Sheri Schmelzer, founder of Jibbitz, used clay and rhinestones to make charms that would fit snugly into the holes of her family's ten pairs of Crocs. An unintentional entrepreneur, Sheri had only made the charms for her own children's shoes but then realised the potential following demand from other inquisitive parents. In December 2006, the Schmelzers realised the fruits of their labour when Crocs, Inc. announced it had acquired Jibbitz LLC to the cool tune of $10 million. www.Jibbitz.com

Allowing consumers the ability to customise standard product purchases is an excellent way to feed off the success of another business. Consider what successful products or services you could support. Imagine stylish silk-screened speaker covers for Apple's new iPod Hi-Fi or fashionable covers to protect your laptop, phone or iPod.

The key to profiting from this trend is to identify a business concept enjoying remarkable success by satisfying customers' needs. Once you have identified this business, you need to ask yourself, 'How can I help support this business?' For example, childcare has become a booming industry. What could you do to help these businesses satisfy the needs of their customers – the caregivers and parents? What does the childcare industry need that it currently lacks or is struggling to cope with? With the current debate about children's health and the need for healthy meals, perhaps you could start a lunch truck business that caters specifically to the staff and children of a childcare centre. If you are able to keep costs down and build a solid client base among carers and parents this could be an ideal way to service the needs of a large, growing industry.

Toy manufacturers are notorious for feeding off the success of other toys, especially licensed characters. For example, you can either purchase the genuine Thomas the Tank Engine train set or you can purchase the Thomas train separately and buy non-genuine train tracks, which do exactly the same job for half the cost – a considerable saving for any parent. Baby Born comes with her own official wardrobe – garments costing the equivalent of a young girl's top. Alternatively, you can turn to eBay to discover that some crafty entrepreneurs have designed and produced their own designer wardrobe for Baby Born, again at a fraction of the cost of the original products.

To demonstrate how easy it is to come up with a business concept that dovetails into the success of another established business, consider the following examples. Each one of these businesses has ridden to success on the coat-tails of another thriving business.

Bemz, a Swedish company, is successfully piggybacking off the success of IKEA. Bemz sells removable, washable slipcovers for sofas, armchairs and cushions. The key to Bemz's success is its focus. Bemz has targeted a niche market – customers who have purchased IKEA sofas, armchairs and cushions. This was a very smart move. Bemz's potential market includes millions of homes around the world furnished by IKEA. www.bemz.com

Funky Fone Sox is feeding off the success of the mobile phone industry. Inspired by co-founder Nicola Vane, they were probably the first in the UK to offer clothes for phones and MP3 players, a mobile phone sock to protect the phone's buttons and screen from getting scratched. It allows people to personalise their phone with cool designs in vibrant colours. They also have a bespoke service for individual requirements. www.funkyfonesox.co.uk

Trend 12: Don't buy it, hire it

Consumers are increasingly opting to rent instead of buy. From handbag subscriptions to baby clothing, businesses are making it possible for consumers to hire instead of investing heavily in a purchase. For consumers, hiring products is the cost-effective alternative to ownership. They are supporting this trend because it allows them the opportunity to experience different products without the cost of ownership and limits the negative impact of making the wrong purchase.

Whether we like it or not, the consumer of today is offered a vast range of choices and experiences. To woo the modern-day consumer, businesses need to consider how they can keep making the purchase of their products fresh and exciting. What business opportunities does this trend create? Here are some great examples of businesses bridging the gap between use and purchase, allowing consumers the opportunity to hire instead of buy.

Carol Wexler founded BorrowedBling.com, where the everyday consumer can enjoy the 'million-dollar celebrity look' for a fraction of the cost. BorrowedBling.com has taken the United States by storm, inviting the public into the inner sanctum of Hollywood and enabling anyone to borrow the same gorgeous jewellery and accessories that television shows and stars have been using for years. BorrowedBling.com offers a new twist on shopping because not only can you buy any of the items seen there, but you are also allowed to borrow or rent them. Where else are you encouraged to wear and then return items? The site has been called a 'shopping fantasy come true' by its loyal members. www.borrowedbling.com

Owning the latest and greatest in designer fashion accessories can be rather difficult on a budget. Jo Trafford is the founder of Handbag Hire HQ, an innovative business helping women keep up with the latest trends by providing an extensive range of handbags for hire. Handbag Hire HQ offer their customers the opportunity to experience the very latest in fashionable luxury handbags at an affordable price. And if parting with the designer bag is just too hard to do, Jo offers the ability through the website to 'acquire' as well as to 'hire' a bag, giving the options to purchase either new or nearly new at a substantially reduced price. www. handbaghirehq.co.uk

Rentoid connects owners and renters of almost anything. Rent anything from anyone. Or have someone rent something from you. A recent entrant in the online world, Rentoid is like eBay but for renting. You might want a ladder and someone in your area might be willing to rent it to you for the weekend for a couple of pounds. The site gets 5 per cent of the transaction. www.rentoid.com

To profit from this trend, take the time to consider what you could rent out. Ideally this would be a product that temporarily provides a solution, such as baby equipment or furniture; it's not like you will need this equipment for the rest of your life. Also consider products that grow old before their time – this is especially the case with modern gadgets. What's in today is out tomorrow so a majority of consumers – particularly tech-savvy consumers and those who want to keep up with the Joneses – would happily rent knowing they could upgrade when necessary. Whilst the concept has been tried and tested with electronic products, consider what other products are equally suitable.

Trend 13: Give me an all-in-one solution

Entice customers with all-in-one solutions that save time and money. Sadly we have become a lazy society and few people are prepared to go shopping for individual items if they can get everything they need through an all-in-one solution. Convenience is key; we like everything right at our fingertips. Consider what products you could market as one-stop solutions that will perfectly satisfy the needs of consumers. The list is extensive, from do-it-yourself gardening kits complete with shovels, gloves, seeds and soil, to make-your-own hot sauce kits with spices, recipes and empty bottles with labels to personalise, or muffin kits with all the ingredients perfectly measured and a tray to bake them in. Virtually any kind of product can be packaged as part of a kit. The trick is finding an all-in-one solution demanded by a group of consumers who would be prepared to pay. So what could you package up?

_ A home brew kit complete with labels, distinctive bottles, and beer holders.
_ A travel kit – with mini shampoo, soap, toothbrush.
_ Wedding day survival kit.
_ Bringing home baby kit.

A great example of a business that has this trend all boxed up is

Splat Cooking. Launched in 2001, the company produces a range of children's cooking kits and cooking party kits specially designed for budding chefs aged five to eighteen. The kits are designed to promote cooking skills, healthy eating and nutritional learning through hands-on participation. The top sellers are kits for pizzas, cookies and cupcakes, with their cookie cutters recognised by top chefs such as Nigella Lawson. www.splatcooking.net Founder Beverley Glock also writes cookery articles for a number of publications and websites including the all-encompassing www.all4kidsuk.com

The Pink Tool Box is another great example of a business that sources a variety of products that are then presented in one convenient kit. The garden kit, for example, is packed with everything the budding green thumb could possibly require to transform anything from a window box to a full flower bed – it even includes hand cream for after the work is done! The Pink Tool Box company clearly targets women and has kits available for the home, car, office and travel. www.pinktoolbox.co.uk

I hope you now have a deeper understanding of some of the trends that exist in our society and, just as importantly, how you can use these trends to develop your own business concept. I also hope the businesses mentioned inspire you to come up with your own idea. But above all remember that your idea need not conquer the world's problems – it need only satisfy a subset of consumer needs. You do not have to reinvent Einstein's theory of relativity. Instead, keep your ideas small and simple

...at least to start with.

I need a business idea

If you are struggling to identify a business opportunity from world trends, don't worry. I have a comprehensive list of ideas to stimulate your creative juices.

Remember, an idea is just a seed. It is what you add to the seed that will see it grow into a sustainable and profitable business. Use the list of ideas as a starting point. Search the web to see what else is out there and how you could add your own unique twist to the idea to differentiate yourself from potential competitors.

Where possible I have discussed the idea in detail, providing reference sites to help demonstrate the potential. Other concepts are short, sharp and to the point as they require less explanation.

1. Handmade soaps, lotions, bath salts, skincare

Handmade soaps and lotions have never gone out of vogue. In 2007, the global market for bath and shower products was £15 billion, of which hand soap made up almost £6 billion and liquid soaps nearly £2 billion, according to Euromonitor figures quoted in the www.cosmeticsbusiness.com article "Bathroom Products - the bare essentials", March 2009. You can really make a go of this business idea on any one of a number of levels. Even if you don't have much experience in this field you certainly will have a great deal of fun experimenting and learning as you go. You can find basic soap and lotion recipes on the Internet or in various magazines. Perhaps you could even experiment making up your own.

You may wish to appeal to a niche market of consumers who have a certain type of skin condition such as eczema or psoriasis. With proper research you might just discover a combination of ingredients that can help ease the suffering of people with this problem.

You could sell soaps at a market stall, in a brown paper bag, no frills, just a wonderful combination of tempting aromas.

You could devise a unique combination of organic scents for a range of skin lotions and soaps packaged in a lavish box. You could also get a little more creative and make your own range of soap shapes, for example ice blocks on a stick, soap cupcakes – a great idea to market to gift givers. With this idea you are only limited by your imagination. Both styles of product would sell well through large department stores or boutique household goods and gift stores.

Your marketing strategy could include the creation of an online 'soap club'. If you sold your soaps through a market stall, you could offer free membership to capture the details of both browsers and paying customers. This is a great way to directly promote your business to potential customers and encourage continued patronage. Given the likelihood of the consumer not returning to the market, providing members with the ability to conveniently reorder soaps and lotions online will help you to maintain sales. Your 'soap club' should provide interesting information that is relevant to the customer's needs. You could even consider providing information on the different soaps that you stock. For example, some of your soaps may aid in relaxation or help to moisturise the skin. To maximise the benefit of this marketing strategy ensure your packaging promotes your 'soap club' and your free offer of membership.

An online 'soap club' will help to increase the avenues through which you could distribute your product. If you only distribute your product through a market stall then the potential of your business is limited geographically to the immediate area and surrounding suburbs.

One entrepreneur who has carved out a profitable niche market in soaps is The Cocoa Shack. This boutique soap company is tucked away on the south coast of England. Their soap is made from a combination of luxury oils and a key ingredient – fresh goat's milk. The Cocoa Shack has proven very popular with people who have sensitive skin, eczema or psoriasis. www.cocoa-shack.co.uk

2. Screen-printing T-shirts

You can literally have anything screen-printed but this idea focuses on T-shirts, a small segment of a much bigger market. To pursue this business idea successfully you should possess some degree of experience in the field of screen-printing. Alternatively you could undertake a short weekend course to develop a basic understanding and refine your skills with practice.

Screen-printing enables you to appeal to a number of potential target markets. There are consumers who purchase specially printed tops as souvenirs; others desire a specific or unique design to reflect a specific occasion, such as a group holiday or team tour. If you have a flair for design, you could opt to target a certain segment of consumers, such as surfers, skaters or children, to name just a few. You could design your own range of tops for toddlers or children, with creative, witty slogans. A range like this could be sold through any distribution channel but boutique retail stores would be ideal. Some UK-based companies experiencing success in the screen-printing industry for kids clothing include www.allthingsgreen.net, www.thekidswindow.co.uk, and www.jklclothing.co.uk.

If you decide to design and screen-print your own range, it's essential that you research what designs appeal to your target market. Don't just design something because you like it. Your target market must like it as well or you won't make sales.

You could consider setting up an online store and hosting a competition for the best design. The design voted the best by visitors to the site would be the design screen-printed and sold for the week. Check out an example below.

The following businesses have taken the concept of screen-printing and added a slight twist.

Reactees are T-shirts designed to ignite a public reaction. The tees themselves are interactive combining fashion, SMS and activism to create 'shirts that text back'. Reactee has combined its experience with the mobile phone industry, consumer Internet and the apparel industry to make T-shirts that bridge the gap between the physical world, mobile communications and the Internet. The T-shirts serve as quirky conversation starters. Individuals and organisations can order T-shirts with their own unique personal slogan, keyword and response, and can also select a colour and size. The customer nominates their mobile phone number so that Reactee can activate the keyword. When someone sees the T-shirt they can send a text message (SMS) with the keyword to the Reactee short code. In return they receive a text message specified by the T-shirt's creator.

What type of consumers are Reactee targeting? Individuals who want to connect to others. Consider this concept in light of the phenomenal success of MySpace, YouTube and so on, and you will see the potential.

Reactee customers include individuals such as DJs who want to share their playlists, political activists promoting a candidate, people who just want to get something off their chest, or organisations that can make many T-shirts with the same keyword and use them to promote their unique cause. www.reactee.com

According to the founders, The T-Shirt Deli was established because they wanted to customise shirts, baby hats, underwear and dog T-shirts in order to make gift giving just as much fun as receiving. The T-Shirt Deli looks exactly like a deli with T-shirts stocked in a large deli counter. Everything can be customised: choose a shirt style and size, select your image or slogan and pick the font that suits you best. The finished product is rolled and wrapped in butcher's paper and served with delicious potato chips. www.tshirtdeli.com

Threadless is an ongoing T-shirt design competition. Four to six designs are chosen every week from 600-plus submissions to be printed and sold from the site with the winning designers receiving $2000 in cash and prizes! The project was started in January 2000 by two Chicago area designers, Jake Nickell and Jacob DeHart. Since then over 450 winning designs have been chosen to be printed from more than 60,000 submissions. The Threadless community is thriving with over 300,000 users signed up to score designs and an average of 3000 more signing up every week! www.threadless.com

3. Wooden Toys

Old-fashioned and vintage stores are making a comeback. It would seem destructible plastic toys don't cut the mustard for some parents. Wooden toys such as train sets, building blocks, cubbyhouse furniture and doll's houses are gaining a greater following.

If you are rather crafty you may wish to save considerable start-up costs and make the toys yourself. Alternatively you could always design a range of toys and have these made or sourced from a supplier.

You could even sell a range of wooden toys in kit form. Imagine a little self-assembled wooden kitchen, including stove, fridge and cupboards. You could well be the next mini-IKEA for kids. With an increase in the demand for cubbyhouses you could consider becoming a mini-interior designer, making kit furniture and appliances to furnish these mini-palaces.

Again there are many distribution channels you could consider to sell this type of product. How you decide to distribute your product really depends upon your ability to secure or produce sufficient stock to fulfil orders. A product range of five to eight different toys will adequately support this type of business – it would be difficult to satisfy the needs of your total target market with just one style or category of toy. I would suggest the ideal distribution channels for this product are:

1. boutique toy and baby stores
2. an online store (possibly eBay)
3. childcare centres
4. party plan.

Since wooden toys are more expensive than plastic ones you would be better off distributing this product through upmarket toy stores whose customers are less price sensitive. If you distributed this type of product through a mainstream department store or discount toy store you would probably need to drop your selling price and that would ultimately impact on your profit margin. Please note, if you sell wooden toys online, your marketing campaign should be designed to drive traffic to your site. I would highly recommend using an affiliated networker like Silvertap or Google's AdWords to build awareness and promote your product range. By employing such online marketing tools you will be able to direct your message to your specific target market. It's pointless wasting your e-advertising spend on broad appeal.

Ensure your products are clearly branded. The parents who have your products will then be directly advertising your product to their friends with children when they play with the toys. Word-of-mouth can be very effective. You want to capitalise on any opportunity to publicise your business brand.

You could also sell your range to childcare centres. The number of childcare centres is growing so there is no shortage of demand for quality, long-lasting toys. Make initial contact with a childcare centre by sending a brochure of your product range and follow up with a phone call to arrange a meeting. You may wish to entice the childcare centre with a special package deal as an introductory offer.

Brickadoo creates toys that enable children to build their own toy house. The toy comes with real building materials – bricks, cement, and wooden windows and doors. Suitable for all ages, this product comes with an added twist: the building blocks can be used again and again because the cement dissolves quickly in water. www.brickadoo.com

For more inspiration, check out the UK site www. sendmetoys.com..

4. Wedding planner

Despite what some magazines would have us believe, marriage is not going out of fashion. Women still want their special day. However, with the pressures of work commitments and a demanding social life, more and more women nowadays are having difficulty finding the time to organise a wedding. If you are an organiser at heart, a business specialising in wedding planning services could be perfect for you.

Becoming a successful wedding planner requires some networking in the industry. Start by identifying and affiliating yourself with some of the bigger players such as florists, chauffeurs and reception centres. If you can create strong working relationships with a number of reputable suppliers, they may agree to recommend your services to the engaged couples they meet.

Your marketing strategy should concentrate on appealing to newly engaged couples – ideally those who are time poor.

You may decide to advertise your services in. *Brides Magazine* or *You & Your Wedding*. In Australia, there is a free magazine, *The Bride's Diary*, that a number of major newspapers give away when a couple places an engagement notice in the newspaper. See if there are similar deals locally. You could also advertise your business on various bridal websites since many engaged couples turn to such websites for ideas, research and basic information.

Find out what wedding competitions are held annually and by whom. Contact the organisers and see if you can offer your services as part of the overall prize. This will help increase the exposure of your business. If you decide to promote your business through the various wedding expos held each year then you will need to have a 'Wow!' factor to woo the couple. Brides and grooms will not consider using you above another wedding planner unless you can think of a creative and unique way to capture their attention.

You could also consider advertising and promoting your services online. There is a host of wedding directory sites catering to brides. It would be a good idea to connect with one or two of these and see if there are any opportunities to act as an online consultant, each week answering one or two questions, or perhaps offering to blog for the site. This will allow you to build a profile and is a cost-effective way to promote yourself as an expert in the field.

5. Arts and crafts supplies

To start this business you must have a passion and flair for arts and crafts. If you are not a creative person your ability to satisfy the needs of your target market will be limited.

Retailing arts and crafts products online is a great way to start your own business. You could specialise in one particular area and serve a niche market such as scrapbooking, special artist paints and canvases, or children's arts and crafts. This is a great business opportunity for anyone who already has a particular interest in the field.

You could decide to specialise in a product range that is difficult to source. If you found a product in another country that would be well accepted in your own, you could contact the supplier and come to an agreement that gave you the sole distribution rights in your country. If you import a range of arts and crafts products you would be better off approaching retail outlets to stock your product list.

If you are starting out with limited funding you may wish to consider using eBay and setting up a store to sell your products. Using eBay provides an optimal means to distribute your product to a worldwide market for relatively little cost.

You could also distribute your products through various market stalls as well as maintaining an online presence either through eBay or with your own site. If you decide to set up your own website, you should create an online craft club, perhaps even add a forum where users can discuss projects they are working on. This is a fantastic way to obtain the contact details of potential purchasers. Once you have a visitor's details you can directly communicate with them through monthly newsletters, promoting specials, package offers and so on. It is far cheaper to target a customer you have already created a relationship with than it is to take a 'pot shot' with a magazine advertisement in the hope that you hit a pool of potential customers.

Other ideas to market this business successfully include holding regular craft classes in your local community. Teaching people how to use your product range to create something will encourage participants to purchase your products at the conclusion of the class. Furthermore the item created becomes a talking point. If you make the classes fun, high-energy and creative you will have participants cheering about your business.

Here's an example of what you could do.

Tai Broadhurst founded The Little Experience after a fruitless search for children's activities that required concentration as well as participation. Tai decided to assemble activity kits for creative projects. Her kits include a range of projects from building a birdhouse to knitting a monkey doll. There are kits for boys and girls all categorised by age group. Each project is designed for fun, while stimulating the curious young mind. www.the-little-experience.com

6. Gourmet herbs

To start this business you won't need acres and acres of land. You can successfully grow a variety of herbs in pots or tubs so you only need a bit of a green thumb and a limited understanding of horticulture. What this business idea really depends on is your ability to grow and sell high quality gourmet herbs to upmarket restaurants, boutique supermarkets or fresh-produce market stalls.

Before you start madly sowing seeds, I recommend consulting chefs from a number of high-class restaurants as these are a key target market. Find out what sort and what quantity of herbs they commonly use and what standard and quality they expect the herbs to be. Do they only use organically grown herbs? Do they have a problem with hydroponics? Talk to as many members of your target market as possible.

Visit potential distributors to see if they already stock supplies of gourmet herbs. If so, what is the standard of their product and how is it packaged? Could you increase the appeal of your product to the end customer if you packaged the herbs differently, perhaps including a recipe incorporating their use?

Research various soils and fertilisers that can affect the growth, quality, colour and taste of the herbs.

Due to the nature of this business your target market would be geographically limited by your ability to deliver the herbs at peak freshness. You would need to identify methods of effectively and efficiently transporting the herbs.

Advertising this business would be of limited value. To generate sales you would need to initially approach your target market in one-on-one sales meetings. It is important to create strong relationships with your customers as they can also help you identify other potential herbs you could supply.

You could also consider selling your herbs through various farmers' markets. These are the latest craze as they cut out the middleman and bring fresh produce to the consumer and are in keeping with the trend towards more sustainable, environmentally friendly practices.

If you think this idea can't be done, check out www.gourmetherbs.com.au and www.ehow.co.uk.

7. Personalised Christmas ornaments

Personalised Christmas ornaments and decorations are very special. They are keepsakes that can adorn the Christmas tree time and time again, handed down for generations and serving as a reminder of family history and heritage.

If you are artistic you may know of a way to make wonderful Christmas ornaments and decorations that can be personalised. You could also source decorations from a supplier and use a unique means to personalise the decoration yourself.

> Make sure the surface of the decoration can be personalised permanently. It would be devastating to your business if the names on your decorations could easily or quickly rub off!

This business would be best operated through a website as this will allow you to target a worldwide market. Again, if funding is limited, use eBay to sell your products and consider developing your own website further down the track. You could also use an order-form system and direct mail to appeal to a local target market.

To market this business you could undertake your own PR strategy – sending samples to various magazines read by your target market. I have done this personally and can vouch for it. It is the most cost-effective marketing strategy I have ever employed.

You could target large businesses, preferably those with 100 to 200-plus employees or clients. Your personalised decorations could be the ideal solution for the company that believes in giving a small gift to their staff or clients at Christmas time.

Besides Christmas decorations for the tree you could extend your product range to include personalised Santa bags, Christmas lollies, table settings, napkins … the list is endless. If you Google 'personalised Christmas ornaments' you will discover there are several online businesses specialising in this product range. Check them out and see how you could go one better.

8. Handbags

Handbags never go out of fashion. It's only the style that changes. If you break the concept of a handbag down to its simplest form, people are buying a means of carrying personal effects. This is any bag's main purpose. Therefore the potential target market could include people looking for an alternative way to carry a laptop, a mobile phone, a PDA, a purse, a wallet, a diary, school or library books or the groceries. Success may be as simple as entering the market with a new and innovatively designed bag that holds such items in a more efficient and effective manner. You might like to consider specialising in a certain type of bag such as nappy bags, evening bags, cocktail party bags, everyday bags or children's handbags.

You could source stock for this business in a variety of ways:

_ You could find a manufacturer (nationally or internationally) who makes the type of bag you believe will satisfy the unmet needs of your group of consumers.
_ You could design a range of handbags and find someone to make the bags according to your designs.
_ You could design and make the bags yourself.

Undertake your own market research. You may find consumers favour a certain style. Your research could also reveal design features or attributes that are missing from the latest ranges of handbags. Find a place where you can observe your ideal target market using their handbags. This may provide you with the inspiration to design a completely new and innovative handbag.

Why not combine the design of a handbag with the use of recyclable materials? Using recyclable raw materials to produce a range of fashionable and stylish handbags will appeal not only to environmentalists but also to those who seek the latest in hip, cool and funky. Not only will you have a distinct point of differentiation, you will also be doing something good for the environment.

9. Printed posters

Any poster first printed more than 70 years ago is classified as in the public domain. This means it is copyright free and you can reprint and sell it. Some amazing artwork is available, including Olympic posters and art exhibit posters as well as material from World War I and before. These beautiful reproduction posters are often used in home decorating. With a website you can start to sell posters worldwide and you don't have to pay any licence fees.

You could even take the poster prints and apply the designs to improve other products; for example, you could recreate a 1923 design and apply it to a range of tea towels, place mats or coasters – the possibilities are endless.

10. Online advertising master

There is an incredible amount of competition on the Internet; the online business owner has to do a lot to attract the attention of potential customers. It can also be expensive to advertise on the Internet as the cost of pay-per-click advertising campaigns has sky-rocketed in line with the demand. For the budding entrepreneur this represents a great opportunity. There are many free online communities, listings and forums you can approach to list your business. However, the average business owner simply doesn't have the time to take advantage of these golden opportunities to drive traffic to their site.

You could offer to help these businesses out and earn extra money online by submitting clients' websites. You could carve out a niche as someone who manually submits people's sites to 50 or 60 of the most important search engines, review sites, forums, relevant listings and directories – all of which will drive traffic back to the business owner's site.

Best of all, this business is transparent. You can show your client exactly where and why you have listed their business on the Internet. I once had a person mention my first book in a forum/chat room. I could see from my Google Analytics report that this mention of my book and link to my site had resulted in over 2500 visits from potential customers.

You should be aware that one of the biggest obstacles facing online business owners is the fact that they cannot easily penetrate forums. If you post a blatant promotional comment to a forum you will more than likely be banned, so you need a neutral third person who has been with the forum for quite some time and has the respect of fellow members. Anyone who has posted over 100 times is never suspected as a promoter; their opinion is generally respected because of their standing as a member. So if you are going to infiltrate forums do so with a great deal of cunning; for example, you can set up multiple memberships – you could be four members in one.

11. Write a book

Could you be the next J.K. Rowling? The creator of Harry Potter has gone from being a single mum struggling to pay the rent to a successful world renowned author with a personal wealth conservatively estimated to be between £600 million and £700 million. Have you ever had a great idea for a book? What expert knowledge do you possess that would be of benefit to someone else? Or do you have an ability to dream up creative and spellbinding plots?

This is a great way to impart your knowledge or creatively generate an income. To be a successful writer the subject of your book must engage the reader. A self-help book, for example, must provide the reader with relevant, practical information that solves a problem.

There are some great books detailing how to write a book, what to include and exclude, as well as how to self-publish your work or appeal to a publisher.

To self-publish successfully you may need to organise the following services:

_ editor
_ designer
_ typesetter
_ indexer
_ photographer
_ illustrator
_ distributing agent.

For example, if you wanted to write a recipe book you might need to team up with a photographer. Likewise if you created a children's book you might need the services of an illustrator. These need not be expensive. You could contact students training in the relevant industry, e.g. graphic arts or photography. Alternatively, you might consider getting in touch with a community arts association to see if there is anyone interested in assisting with your project. You could possibly discover a stay-at-home mum who could provide you with the services you are looking for. Ideally you should try to target people prepared to work for 'love money'. This is where someone is happy to work on your project for free under an agreement that when it becomes profitable they receive payment for their services.

If you decide to self-publish you will need to be very creative in the ways you distribute the book. One of the main advantages of using a publisher is that they will organise and control the distribution of the book. However, if you can't find a publisher and decide to self-publish you will need to devise a strategy to get your book into the hands of your target market. For example, you may decide to create a range of children's books and sell them through a party-plan arrangement, online or through gift shops. You could consider approaching a major corporation to co-sponsor the book. This is an ideal situation especially if there is a marketing angle for the sponsor – a manufacturer of baby food might be interested in financially backing a book aimed at parents and focused on coping with fussy eaters.

The cost of self-publishing could be minimised by offering various businesses an opportunity to advertise in the book. For example, if you decided to produce a cookbook, you could offer advertising space to companies who manufacture the ingredients used in the featured recipes.

12. Client Relationship Management

Businesses need to compete on more than just the merits of their product or service if they want to woo and retain their client base. Client Relationship Management (CRM) is a service that has been born out of the increasingly competitive environment in which most businesses now operate. It has long been known in the business world that it costs more to appeal to and secure a new customer than it does to retain an existing one.

CRM gives rise to a great idea for a home-based business tailor-made for anyone who enjoys organisational and administrative work. Many businesses would ideally love to outsource CRM activities such as sending out monthly newsletters, co-ordinating marketing campaigns, dealing with customer feedback forms, and so on. There are very few businesses servicing the CRM needs of small business, so competition in this area is relatively low. A great feature of this idea is that you can literally target any business that has customers – doctors, dentists, accountants, portrait and wedding photographers, hairdressers, plumbers and other trade businesses. In addition, it requires hardly any set-up costs. Basically all you need is a computer, an Internet connection and a great sales pitch to take to your potential customers.

A perfect example of the need for CRM is in the property industry. While some estate agents now have CRM systems in place, all too often you hear of situations where the estate agent is the vendor's best friend during the sale of the property but never makes contact with the vendor or even remembers their face once the property is sold. With effective CRM, the agent would have been able to maintain contact with the vendor so that when they were ready to sell another property that agent would be the first person they'd call. Alternatively the vendor might be asked to recommend the name of a reliable estate agent. If the agent maintained contact then it's more than likely that the vendor would recommend them.

In essence CRM involves maintaining contact with clients to encourage repeat business. Businesses need to maintain and manage the relationships they have with their current clients so that these clients don't revert to a competitor. Businesses are more profitable when they gain leverage from their current client base. Unfortunately most businesses are focused on day-to-day operational activities and simply don't have the time or resources to devote to CRM.

Your service range could include the following activities:

_ sending out monthly newsletters
_ co-ordinating and mailing out various gifts to clients on occasions such as their birthday or the anniversary of a major purchase
_ organising client reminders
_ co-ordinating service evaluation forms and feedback
_ distributing Christmas gifts or other promotional products to clients
_ maintaining and updating the client database.

There are many more services you could offer to help businesses add value and maintain their relationship with their clients. Consider your own situation. How would you feel if your hairdresser sent you a voucher on your birthday, or if your dentist sent you a reminder that it was time for your annual check-up?

Effective CRM will ensure the consumer is subtly reminded of the business's services on a regular basis, so when they need such a service again your client's business is their first port of call.

There are already CRM-based businesses operating – you can

find these on the Internet. However, most of these businesses cater for larger clients with a greater customer base. There is a very viable niche in the CRM market catering to the needs of smaller businesses. You could target those small businesses that recognise their marketing strategy should incorporate a service focused on maintaining client contact and generating referrals.

13. Desktop publishing

If you have some experience in the field of graphic design or are a qualified graphic artist, why not offer a desktop publishing service? Desktop publishing involves the design and creation of various documents such as business cards, letterheads, brochures, catalogues, booklets – anything that requires some form of image or graphics. It's a great home-based business as you can effectively choose your own hours, even working at night if you prefer.

There are several target markets for this business. You could consider targeting only government organisations and departments, as they typically produce an amazing number of brochures, handouts and other reading material. Alternatively, you might decide to target smaller businesses such as takeaway restaurants, hairdressers or tradespeople who cannot afford to use the services of more expensive graphic designers operating out of an office or design studio. Or you might go for broke and pitch your services to a large national business in the hope of gaining wide exposure. You could even consider offering your services to local printers who might have excess workload.

To kick-start sales you should meet with various potential clients to present and showcase your artistic talents. You will need to have some experience in design packages such as Adobe InDesign, but the good news is that you can easily attend a three-day course to get yourself up to speed.

While many designers charge a high fee for their work, the success of this business idea lies in targeting a market of business owners who cannot readily afford the big name designers. You may have to lower your margins, but there is an old saying that you can catch more flies with honey than with vinegar – if you charge a lower price, you will appeal to a larger number of small business owners whose needs and expectations will not be as great. There is a range of small business networks you could tap into with a view to marketing your services.

14. Events co-ordinator

An events co-ordinator is someone who organises various events on behalf of another person or organisation. Corporations in particular use the services of event managers and co-ordinators as they don't have the time or resources to arrange one-off events such as product launches, end-of-year parties, business anniversaries or milestone celebrations.

A business specialising in event management is based around the core skill of organisation. Conduct some market research to find out what the current unmet needs of your potential target market are. What do they expect from an events co-ordinator? Are there any gaps where you could effectively offer a differentiated service and increase your appeal to the target client?

Familiarise yourself with the top venues, reception centres and restaurants in your state or area. You might need to know what's hot in town and what's not in order to be able to provide a high-class experience. Potential clients would expect you to be able to provide all sorts of fresh, creative and unique ideas for their events and celebrations, and it is very important for the success of your business that you are able to respond quickly to their needs.

You could extend your service range by offering to organise corporate seminars and conferences, including inter-regional trips for the sales team. This service would appeal to many medium businesses. Instead of adding to the current workload of staff they could simply outsource the organisation of the conference to your business.

Your services could also extend to trade shows. It is very expensive for companies to participate in trade shows if the show is located a great distance from the company's headquarters. Getting employees to the show two or three days before the start to deal with the last-minute details is also expensive and inconvenient. You can help companies by providing local support for their exhibit at the trade show.

To promote this side of your event co-ordination business, find out what shows are coming to hotels and convention centres in your town, and contact the exhibitors in advance of the show. The list of exhibitors and sponsors can usually be found on the trade show's website. Offer to become their local eyes, ears and hands at the location. When setting your rates, keep in mind that an advance party will cost several thousand pounds in expenses for the extra day or two. A good job done here should result in regular repeat business. Don't forget to pass out your business card and brochure to the other exhibitors while you are setting up!

As a sideline you could also specialise in organising birthday parties. As with any business idea, review the level of competition first. Find out what competitors do and don't do. Is there a niche in the market you could cater to and successfully satisfy the needs of this particular group? This is another service that would appeal to those who are time poor or who can't be bothered dealing with all the frustration and challenges associated with creating a great celebration or event.

An events management business would certainly be a fun business to get into as you would be able to organise fabulous parties using someone else's money. What could be better! However, you would need to be able to handle the stress that accompanies this type of work. Ultimately you would be responsible for ensuring the party or event was a smash hit. This business is ideal for anyone who wants a home-based business, as a lot of the work is centred on organising the various elements that combine to create a successful event: ensuring invites are sent out, planning table and seating arrangements, organising caterers, selecting menus, and so on. Much of this can be done over the phone and via email or fax.

15. Gift baskets and hampers

This is a long-established business concept and there are several reasons why it has been around for some time. Gift basket/hamper businesses offer an alternative gifting solution. An employer may consider giving a hamper to staff at Christmas time. Someone may use the services of a gift basket/hamper business if they wanted to send a gift to a new mum or a sick friend or relative in hospital. They're also a great option for anyone wanting to send a gift rather than flowers. Finally, people might like to send a gift basket as a birthday present.

If you like the idea of creating novel and beautiful gift baskets and hampers then this could be the business for you. But first you need to research what is already available on the market. What are other gift basket/hamper businesses currently doing and why? Which target market will you appeal to? Will you target large corporate businesses, i.e. annual hampers, the general public or both? It is important to identify which target market you intend to pursue as the needs of corporate clients and the general public can differ greatly.

The success of this type of business depends on two factors:

1. the contents of the gift baskets and hampers
2. building up a client base so you are able to gain market access and referrals.

I urge you to do as much research as possible on what you will stock in the hampers before you start the business. To be successful you will need to think outside the square to come up with unique and innovative product offerings. The contents of the basket must provide a compelling reason for someone to want to give you their business rather than your competitor. You may want to consider undertaking some direct market research. Ask friends what they would like to receive in a gift basket from a friend for their birthday. If you have friends who are mothers maybe you could ask them what they would have appreciated in a gift basket while they were in hospital with their new baby.

Consider, for example, the growing acceptance of the effectiveness of natural and herbal remedies in treating common illnesses and ailments. There has been a surge in the number of naturopaths opening shopfronts similar to a doctor's surgery or medical offices. You could possibly team up with a naturopath to devise various gift packs that would include natural and herbal remedies and lotions and maybe even vitamin tablets. I can recall my husband applying a dose of arnica soon after I gave birth to my first child. Arnica is a natural remedy used to help body tissue recover from trauma. It helps relieve bruising, stiffness and muscle soreness. Perhaps you could put together a 'postnatal survival kit'.

If you are going to pursue the general public make sure your marketing strategy is in line with the contents of the basket/hamper. For example, if you are selling baskets full of yummy goodies to take on a picnic then you should advertise through a boutique food store and offer to leave a hamper on display. You could arrange with the food store to put some of their products in the baskets in exchange for shop space. If the food store distributes a monthly newsletter ask if you can feature in it. If you live near a popular tourist or holiday spot, you might consider asking the various accommodation providers and tourist information centres to promote your products.

If you decide to pursue corporate clients I would strongly suggest you speak to these businesses directly. You need to find out what they want in a hamper that they would give to staff and what they would expect to pay for a given number of hampers. Perhaps ask if you could survey the employees to gain their feedback. Once you have ascertained how you could fulfil the needs of the target market then put together a powerful marketing campaign and start to approach various businesses with your range of hampers. In order to secure business in the case of Christmas hampers you might want to offer potential customers a reason to act early and place an order before the Christmas rush, i.e. a discount on making a purchase or placing an order before the end of September. An advantage of pursuing the corporate market with a Christmas hamper is that you are able to secure orders pre-Christmas, making it easier to organise stock and negotiate prices with your suppliers.

16. Children's clothing

The demand for children's clothing is one that's not about to suddenly dry up. Children will always need clothes and more babies are always being born. However, to enter the children's clothing industry successfully you must be creative and your clothing range must target a specific need. After all a T-shirt is a T-shirt in any language. If you decided to sell children's T-shirts you would have to consider what made your range of T-shirts so different that a consumer would switch brands to yours.

If you think outside the square you could discover there are niche markets within the overall target market for children's clothing that you could effectively exploit to establish a very successful business. Consider those children born with sensitive skin or conditions such as eczema. For these children some fabrics, particularly polyesters, further exacerbate the problem. You might find there is a genuine market for specialised clothing made from non-allergenic and hyposensitive fabrics. For example, organic cotton and fabrics with aloe vera woven into them are now available.

Every year thousands of babies are born prematurely. The size of such babies means they have clothing needs different from those of full-term babies – there is great demand for tiny hats and jumpsuits.

On the other hand the number of overweight children, some

suffering from the early onset of obesity, is growing. These children need fashionable and stylish clothing, but few clothing retailers specialise in well-designed clothing in extra-large sizes for young people. This is also a great opportunity to build the self-esteem of extra-large children who would no doubt appreciate clothing that helped them feel like other children and assimilate with their peers.

You can source your stock in a number of ways depending on the niche market you decide to serve.

_ You could source clothing made by a national or international supplier.
_ You could design you own range and organise to have it made by an external manufacturer.
_ You could design and make the clothing yourself, provided you have professional sewing skills.

If you decide you are capable of designing and producing your own clothing range, you could enter the market providing limited-edition clothing. This is an idea that works best through a website. You create a limited range of clothing items and make them available on your website. Each week or fortnight you create and promote prototypes of three to four new items of clothing – perhaps a skirt, pants and matching top. These items are available for one or two weeks only. Orders are taken and filled within the following week. One of the best features of this idea is that you only need to purchase the raw materials based on the orders you receive; there's no wastage since you know exactly what is required to make up the week's orders. Your website must provide visitors with an opportunity to submit their details and sign up to receive the weekly newsletter notifying them of the next week's specials. This idea has particular merit as it offers customers the opportunity to purchase unique pieces of clothing unlike the mass-produced items available in department stores. This idea would work just as well for adult clothing.

If you are going to enter a competitive industry such as children's clothing, it's important do so with a clearly differentiated product. Consider the brand t4tot 'hidethatspot'. Rather than enter the already flooded children's clothing industry with a range of stylish and fashionable clothing, innovative mum Samantha Cornish thought outside the square and came up with a fantastic product that truly satisfies consumer's needs within the target market for children's clothing. Samantha developed and designed a fun, fresh and contemporary range of hidethatspot iron-on transfers. She was inspired to create her iron-on transfers by the frustration of toddler spills and spots that just wouldn't come out in the wash, effectively ruining the appearance of an otherwise perfectly good piece of clothing. Samantha says that after endless scrubbing and soaking there always seemed to be those stubborn little stains that remained. She realised, 'If I can't remove them, then why not hide them and at the same time create a fun new look!' and so the idea for t4tot and the range of hidethatspot products was born.

At Huggalugs they put a new twist on stockings-cum-socks and in August 2006 launched their first product: leg and arm 'huggers' (aka leg warmers) for babies and children. The huggers are an original take on an old idea and solve a common problem experienced by all parents. **www.huggalugs.com**

17. Photo restoration

With the large number of photographic software packages around, there is no shortage of means to adapt, enhance and modify photographs. This technology has given rise to another opportunity that is perfect for a home business – photo restoration. If you are confident in your restoration abilities consider what equipment and software you will require.

> It is important that you are the licensee for
> any software you use in your business.

Equipment you will need could include:

_ a scanner – preferably a high-quality negative and print scanner
_ a photo-restoration software program such as Adobe Photoshop
_ a high-quality printer if you are not outsourcing your printing needs.

To market this type of business you might consider teaming up with your local photographic developer or photo lab and offering a complementary arrangement in exchange for the promotion of your services to their customers. This could include the distribution of a flyer with photographs that have been printed by the lab.

You could also design a number of stands advertising your services and pay to have these displayed at various shopping centres.

The ideal target market for this business is baby boomers; they are accustomed to SLR cameras and probably have hundreds of printed photographs. To reach these consumers, you could consider affiliating your services with businesses such as those who specialise in researching and identifying family trees. You may also consider targeting consumers in the more affluent suburbs as, generally speaking, these people have extra disposable income and might also be interested in restoring important moments from their past captured on film. You could approach these potential customers through a well-designed brochure that illustrates your talents.

If you are more adept at using photographic software you might consider extending your services to include the design and printing of photographic montages. A photographic montage is a print made up of a number of photos all elegantly and professionally placed to create one image that is then printed. It's an excellent way to capture a child's first five years for example. Offering to design and print photographic montages is a cost-effective service as, ultimately, the only costs are your time and the printing, both paid for by the customer.

Alternatively you might consider incorporating your photo restoration services with the design and production of photo books. Websites such as www.cewe-photobook.co.uk or www. xbook.com.au provide users with the technology and means to create beautiful photographic books, perhaps depicting someone's life story – the digital alternative to scrapbooking. Users can place an order for one book or twenty, and even place repeat orders. This is a product many people would cherish; however, due to busy schedules, it might not be possible for time-poor people to do it themselves. Instead, they would happily pay someone else to create such a keepsake.

18. Recipes for dog and cat food

Many pet owners treat their dogs and cats like members of the family. It seems reasonable to assume this market of potential customers would take an interest in what they feed their pets. You could tap into pet owners' desire to do the best for their dogs or cats with a recipe book that caters to these pets. All the recipes should contain ingredients already found in people's kitchens or that can be purchased very inexpensively. Make sure the recipes are healthy and can be made in large quantities and frozen for convenience. You could even provide the nutritional content of each recipe as many women's magazines do for theirs. There are many pet magazines on the market where you could promote your product.

You might also like to consider starting a website, where for a membership fee you could provide the customer with access to your stockpile of recipes. From here it would be a matter of promoting your site online and I would recommended you do this by linking to as many related sites as possible. All you need to do is identify the sites you would like to be linked with and then send an email offering a reciprocal link. Linking your site to other sites increases its search engine ranking and is a great way to increase awareness. Blogging is another cost-effective way to create a following of loyal customers. You can start a free blog at www.wordpress.com.

Make sure you capture the names and email addresses of visitors to your site. Irrespective of whether a visitor signs up for your membership, it is very important to maintain your contact with them, perhaps through a monthly newsletter featuring a new recipe or useful nutritional tips. This will ensure your business stays at the forefront of the consumer's mind.

Write to the pet magazines on the market to let them know of your existence. They might offer you a page to promote your recipes or at least feature your business in some small way.

19. Collectables and memorabilia

If you are interested in collectables and memorabilia you may wish to consider starting a business that sells such items. If you already have an interest in this area then this is an added bonus, as you will share a common interest with your target market, making it easier to relate to them. You may decide to stock a number of different categories of collectables or you may decide to specialise in one particular category, such as old teddy bears.

Some other examples of collectables are dolls; art prints; furniture; military items; model cars, planes and trains; books and maps, sheet music and old records; bottles; photographic equipment; china, porcelain and ceramics; old radios, TVs and phonographs; clocks and other timepieces; stamps and coins; phone cards and swap cards; old photographs and postcards.

As you can see from the list above the items that can fall under the umbrella of collectables and memorabilia are endless. You could sell memorabilia through a website, eBay, eBid in the UK or possibly a market stall. There may even be various 'fairs' in your region that allow buyers and sellers of collectables to meet.

You will need to ensure you have a thorough appreciation and in-depth knowledge of the collectables you choose to deal in. When buying stock you need to identify what will sell and what won't, as the success of your business will depend on your ability to spot a bargain that will resell well.

You may purchase stock for this business through:

_ deceased estates
_ second-hand shops
_ garage sales
_ antique stores
_ charity functions – these often sell sporting and other memorabilia in an effort to raise funds.

Collectables can be marketed to both collectors and upmarket homemakers looking for more unusual or exquisite items to furnish and decorate their homes. These consumers usually have a high level of disposable income to justify such purchases.

How you market your business will greatly depend on the type of collectables or memorabilia you decide to stock or specialise in. There are many associations and clubs for various collectables and affiliating yourself with these is an optimal way to directly reach your target market.

This is yet another example of a business that would benefit greatly from effectively managing and marketing the client database. You could establish a website with your own online club to provide the visitor with a compelling reason to leave their details.

It's also a business that allows you to provide customers with an 'extra', which makes them more likely to remember you and use your services in the future. Have fact sheets prepared to send to the client with lots of valuable and helpful information. For example, if you were a coin collector it would be helpful to know the tricks for cleaning coins and tips on storing them.

20. Counsellor

If you are a sensitive and caring person, you could establish a business as a counsellor. Counselling offers many varied fields. You could specialize in counselling children, teenagers, people with marriage problems, or drug or alcohol problems. Since a majority of people work during the day or attend school you will find many of your clients might prefer to make appointments in the evening or on weekends.

Before you open your door to take on the worries of the world you will need to review the necessary laws and regulations governing the role of a counsellor. You should check with your local council to find out if you need a licence or permit to use your premises to conduct counselling sessions. You will definitely need to be qualified. Do some research to discover what qualifications are required for you to specialise in a particular area of counselling. Your target market will be interested in your qualifications and level of expertise.

Depending on the nature of your counselling service, you could promote your business in your local newspaper or consider affiliating with similar businesses. For example, some couples experiencing marriage problems might consult their doctor for advice. If you could connect with the doctors operating in your area, you could organise for them to refer your counselling services or distribute a brochure on your behalf. If you decide to counsel teenagers or children you could contact the schools in your local area to offer your services.

21. Landscape designer

While many home owners are more than happy to get out in the garden and exercise their green thumb, some don't know what to plant where. If you have experience and expertise in landscape design, you could offer this service to budding green thumbs and advise them on which plants are suitable for their needs, how to care for their garden and why you recommend the various plants and design features. Conditions will vary from garden to garden, so what will thrive in one may not do as well in another. This is where you can really add value, explaining and guiding the choices the home owner makes. Word will soon spread when your client proudly shows off their garden to their neighbours, friends and family.

To further market your business, it would be a good idea to team up with several nurseries. This arrangement benefits both parties. You get more customers while the nursery benefits from increased sales when your clients make the purchases you recommend.

One of the most appealing features of this business is the fact that you have the chance to get leverage from your money-making opportunity. You could offer to simply design the client's garden and leave them to implement the design or, for an extra fee, you could offer to do the actual planting and landscaping work for the client too.

22. Outsourced payroll

Small- to medium-sized businesses generally manage their own payroll. Business owners report this is often a hassle and can lead to a lack of privacy, as it is relatively easy for who earns what to become common knowledge.

If you have had payroll experience you could offer your services as an outsourced payroll officer. Each pay period you would be responsible for administration of the payroll. To get started you would need to make appointments with your ideal clients, presenting your services and demonstrating why your services are required. Importantly, you would need to impress upon any potential client your high levels of integrity and confidentiality as most business owners will want to know that details such as pay rates, bonuses and so on will be kept strictly confidential. I recommend before you meet with potential clients you have a procedure and system documented in a brochure that you can hand out.

To get this business going I suggest you target potential clients who, because of their size, cannot afford a corporate payroll service. For example, the owner of a busy hairdressing salon is typically also one of the hairdressers and is therefore likely to appreciate the opportunity to hand over time-consuming administrative tasks such as payroll management.

23. Bookkeeping service

Do you have a knack for numbers? If you have experience keeping accounts or have worked as a qualified accountant or bookkeeper you could start your own business maintaining the books for a variety of businesses. (If you don't have the necessary formal qualifications, seek out a registered training facility.)

You will need accounting software, and the two main software packages used by accounting firms and recommended for small businesses are MYOB (Mind Your Own Business) and QuickBooks. A bookkeeping service is a great business for an at-home mum. If you have a computer then, apart from the initial investment in the necessary software, there are really very few start-up costs involved and the ongoing costs are minimal. Your bookkeeping service could include managing the clients' paperwork, invoices and other relevant documentation at the end of each fortnight, or monthly. You could prepare the necessary accounts and other applicable statements and reports at the end of each month or quarter depending on the agreement you have with your clients.

The success of this business depends on targeting businesses that need your services and can see the real benefits for their business. You need to think strategically. Choose the businesses that you would like as clients. You may wish to target smaller local businesses, especially trade-based businesses such as plumbers, panel-beaters or electricians who generally are only too happy to outsource their accounting burden.

Go directly to the source and approach them in a service-friendly manner. Don't waste money on expensive advertising in flashy trade magazines where, once again, you may not successfully hit your target clients.

To build a clientele it is also important to network. Contact various associations and trade organisations to whom similar businesses belong. For example, reputable photographers in the UK are members of the Association of Photographers. You could organise to host a presentation to the members of these associations and trade organisations with the aim of indirectly promoting your business.

Finally make it easy for the potential client. Don't charge by the hour but set a flat fee for various services. One of the biggest gripes businesses tend to have with professionals such as accountants is that they charge by the hour and who really knows how much time was actually spent completing the job. If you have a set fee structure clients can easily identify the cost and reconcile the value of your service with what they receive for their money.

24. Grant/tender proposal writer

Writing proposals applying for grants and tendering for government business can be very time consuming, especially for those who have little experience in this area. Businesses in pursuit of government contracts are usually required to submit detailed proposals for projects and it is absolutely vital that these proposals are well-written and professionally presented documents. Writing and formatting such proposals is a highly specialised area, so you would need to have prior experience.

Opportunities to submit tenders are typically published in the newspaper. Work out which businesses would apply for these tenders and then target them as potential clients.

25. Importation broker

If you have worked in importation or have experience in importing goods, why not use this skill to your advantage? This business concept is particularly suited to those who have solid experience and a network of overseas contacts as you will need to understand not only the ins and outs of importing, the relevant laws and associated government charges, but also who the more reputable overseas manufacturers are.

Your clients will look to you to advise them and hold their hand every step of the way. You could offer two services: a full service, where you import the goods on the client's behalf, or an advisory service where you explain to the client what they need to do and coach them through the process. The potential target market for this business is huge. Many budding entrepreneurs have great ideas but struggle to get their business off the ground because of limited connections with the right manufacturers. Generally speaking, manufacturing in the UK or any Western country can be quite expensive. It is well known that China and surrounding countries provide the best opportunities to manufacture a product cost-effectively. However, if you have no contacts in that country, how do you know who to speak to or who is reliable? This is precisely why an importation broker can be so valuable.

To market your idea, start connecting with budding entrepreneurs. Join various networks and get your name out there. You could create a basic website providing the customer with information on what they need to consider before importing – possible government charges and duties or what laws apply and when, for example. Your website should provide just enough information for the customer to see why a broker is so important to the success of their supply chain.

You could also consider appealing to smaller businesses owners who by themselves do not have the ability to capitalise on the low production costs in China. Most major manufacturers ask their customers to order a minimum quantity, but for the small business owner this is often unachievable. However, as part of your business you could effectively bring together several similar smaller businesses to make up an order, thereby making it financially viable for all.

One person who has certainly made this business idea work is Lindy Chen, founder and Managing Director of ChinaDirect Sourcing Services, and author of *Import From China: How To Make A Million ... and Not Get Burnt!* She formed ChinaDirect in 2005 to assist Australian companies to see China not as a threat but as their competitive advantage. In only three years she has saved her clients over $2million in costs. In 2008, ChinaDirect was the winner of the Business Services category of the Australian Small Business Champion Awards for Queensland, and in 2007 won the Australian Home-Based Business Awards www.importingfromchina.com.au. You could check out the China Britain Business Council for more information about importing to the UK. www.cbbc.org

26. The baby planner

These days expecting parents are working right up to the birth of their child. They just don't have the time or energy to trudge from store to store searching for all the items they need to accommodate the birth of their baby. After all, who wants to deal with all that endless, well-meaning advice, which usually only serves to confuse the vulnerable parent-to-be? Career-oriented parents-to-be are time poor but generally have a high level of disposable income so they can afford to pay someone to deal with the shopping, research, conflicting advice and general stress and confusion that accompanies a first-time pregnancy.

As a baby planner you could offer to take care of many aspects of the imminent arrival – dispel common myths, alleviate confusion and provide independent advice. You could explain to your clients what they need right now and why and what they may need as the baby grows. You could extend your services by offering to help first-time parents settle into their new roles of mother and father. A great example of this business idea operates in the United Kingdom: **www.babyplanners.co.uk**.

The potential of this idea is similar to that of a wedding planner. Just as time-poor, career-oriented couples are turning to the services of a wedding planner to organise the biggest day of their lives, it's not too hard to conceive that this same target market will be looking for a similar service when parenthood approaches.

To be successful in this business you would need to create a network of experts who could give valuable, reputable advice on a range of baby-related subjects, including how and where to exercise during pregnancy, what equipment to buy, nutritional advice and so on.

To market this business, I would recommend you go online as many new mothers readily turn to the Internet for advice. You could also consider blogging on pregnancy and parenting sites, if you can – the aim is to build a profile as an 'expert'. If you have the right credentials and qualifications, such as a certificate in childcare or midwifery expertise, you could consider approaching morning TV shows and offering to appear as their resident baby planner. Alternatively you could approach various parenting magazines with a stock of articles based around the concept 'what to consider when you are having a baby'.

27. Bed and bath

The trend for DIY renovations and landscaped gardens has spilled over into the bedroom and bathroom, where homemakers are now seeking the designer look. This has resulted in a significant demand for quality bed and bathroom linen and accessories. There is a target market of consumers who desire the bedrooms and bathrooms featured in the major lifestyle magazines. This opens up a viable opportunity to establish a business that both designs and sells bed and bathroom linen, including accessories such as duvet covers, pillowcases, sheets, valances, bath towels, hand towels, face washers and bath mats.

You could design your own bed and bathroom linen in a number of ways. For example, you could buy a number of duvet covers in various plain colours and use fabric paints to paint on various designs. Alternatively, you might consider creating and attaching various patchwork designs to give a 'shabby chic' appearance. Craft and fabric stores stock an array of products that could be used to enhance the appearance of any plain item. The ultimate product is a one-off, handcrafted, designer duvet cover!

You might consider designing and making your own linen or you could outsource the production to a textile manufacturer. Compare the costs and profit margins for each option.

A handcrafted duvet cover, for example, is unique. Its individuality means you can charge a premium selling price. As your ideal target market consists of individuals seeking the designer look, they too will be prepared to pay the premium price. Your packaging must also reflect the exceptional quality of your product. Your target customer will use it to judge the quality of the item inside since they probably won't be able to open the packaging prior to purchase. So think carefully about unique and fun packaging concepts you could use to capture their attention.

There are a few distribution channels you could consider selling your product through. Boutique bed and bathroom linen stores are an obvious choice as these are where your target market is likely to shop. A stall at a premium market is another option, as some members of your target market will certainly shop at various boutique markets. Again, packaging is the key.

Furniture, bedding and bathroom showrooms are excellent locations to sell premium linen. The customer can see the product on a bed or in a bathroom. They can touch and feel it. When buying a new bed or renovating a bathroom people also like to buy new linen to complement their purchase. I recommend you allow the stores to display your stock on a consignment basis, whereby you don't receive payment until the store sells the stock.

To market your product range successfully you could also display it at various expos, particularly those that retailers from major stores attend to purchase stock.

Here is an example of a business that spotted this opportunity. Inmod, based in New Jersey, is empowering their customers with the opportunity to design their own bed linen. Inmod Design Studio™ allows customers the creative freedom to design their own luxury bedding. Customers can choose from dozens of fabrics and embroidery colours, and a growing selection of chic modern, retro, pop-art, geometric and nature-inspired designs. Inmod's custom bedding is hand-embroidered and crafted from premium fabrics

including silk taffeta, silk dupioni, and a plush linen blend.
www.inmod.com

28. Maternity wear online library

Maternity wear is one of those purchases that you have to make whether you want to incur the expense or not. One of the main problems with maternity wear, apart from the fact that it is generally expensive, is that it is difficult to get your money's worth. Before you know it you are no longer pregnant and you may have only worn the item for four months or so. By the time you need to wear maternity clothes again chances are the fashionable items you spent so much money on are now out of date.

This business idea involves satisfying the needs of those who don't want to spend a great deal on maternity wear; however, perhaps due to their profession, they need to remain fashionable and stylish while pregnant. Establishing an online 'maternity wear hire service', where pregnant women can pay a membership fee to use the clothing for a period of time and then return it, is an idea based on the principles of the handbag business Handbag Hire HQ. www.handbaghirehq.co.uk

This concept is similar to a library. Items of clothing are loaned out for a certain period of time for a set fee depending on the period the clothing is borrowed for and the number of items involved. Women could opt to hire a pair of pants for one month or four depending on their needs.

The idea is particularly endearing because it also lends itself to other business ventures run in conjunction with it. Once you have established a website and have a high level of traffic visiting your site you could offer to sell advertising space to other businesses with a similar target market.

To market this business successfully you will need to build a database capturing the details of visitors to the site. Marketing to your database each month will help build word-of-mouth and increase brand recognition.

Because this business concept is relatively unique and new to the market, I recommend you use a reputable public relations agent or, if you have experience in PR, consider undertaking your own media campaign. You can gain a great deal of free advertising when your business is featured in the media; however, media interest largely depends on the uniqueness of your business idea.

To establish this business you should consider the following:

_ Developing a website that has the following functions: online membership registration and a credit card payment facility.
_ Making sure you have adequate storage space for your stock.
_ Establishing a good relationship with a courier service.
_ Creating a business relationship with a drycleaner, as the garments will need to be dry-cleaned before they are hired out again.
_ Finding out about any relevant health and safety regulations.

To minimise the cost of buying stock, seek out factory outlets or buy directly from manufacturers.

29. Cakes

Do you have a talent for producing scrumptious cakes? Then why not share your delights and establish a business that specialises in producing cakes for weddings, birthday parties or other special occasions.

You could target a number of markets with a range of delicious cakes. Some cafés don't have the time, expertise or ability to bake quality cakes in-house. To differentiate your product from suppliers that might currently sell to these cafés you need to produce a range of unique and differentiated cakes. Perhaps you could use organic ingredients, gluten-free recipes or develop an innovative range with a combination of ingredients that gives a distinct flavour and texture.

Start by focusing on a number of cafés within a certain geographical area – for example, cafés and restaurants within a 3-mile radius of the town centre. Consider sending complimentary small versions of your cakes to potential customers. While this approach to generating sales is a little time consuming and expensive, it is nevertheless a great way to initiate a relationship with a potential customer and get honest feedback about your product and service.

You could choose to target consumers in the lucrative wedding industry or children's birthday parties, while an alternative target market for this idea is the corporate market. Many businesses in the town centre will purchase cakes to celebrate special occasions. One business in London has already tapped into the needs of this market. Fru Fru specialises in delivering homemade cupcakes decadently decorated with butterflies, daisies and stars, and packaged in black boxes tied with fuchsia ribbons. www.frufru.co.uk

With the right attention to taste and detail this is a relatively easy business idea to get off the ground.

If you really wanted to get creative, consider focusing on novelty cakes. Two companies that have embraced this idea are The Fairy Cake Mother (www.thefairycakemother.co.uk) and Sugar Art (www.michellesugarart.co.uk). Specialising in novelty cakes will certainly provide your business with a real point of difference. Imagine presenting a novelty cake to a café to sell: it would certainly get the café customers talking, building the profile of both the café and your business.

You will need to look into any health regulations governing where and how the cakes can be made.

30. Dried herbs and spices

Most people think that the big brands have cornered the market for herbs and spices. This is not necessarily the case. The large food producers may have the supermarkets covered, but there are other avenues of distribution that have not been infiltrated by the bigger players. You could start a business that sells herbs and spices serving a niche market – gourmet foodies.

You could buy herbs and spices in bulk, then re-package them in stylish and fashionable containers. You could even experiment with combinations of herbs and spices to create exotic, aromatic and flavoursome mixes for a variety of meals, such as meat rubs, marinades and bases for stock. To put a unique spin on your product range you could create a special range of herbs and spices to be used for medicinal purposes, as long as you had appropriate qualifications. Certain herbs and spices have long been used by various cultures to assist in the alleviation of a number of minor medical conditions, including weight loss.

A key factor to success in this business is packaging. How you package the product will dictate where you are able to effectively distribute it. If you package the product in a grand manner you will be able to distribute the herbs and spices through gourmet food stores, upmarket delis and grocery stores and even giftware stores, including online. The consumer who frequents a gourmet food store, as opposed to the supermarket, will more than likely be prepared to pay a premium price for their purchases. In return they expect their purchases to deliver more than just a great flavour. In the context of this idea the customer is not just buying quality ingredients and a means to improve the taste of their cooking, they are also buying something that will look good sitting on the kitchen bench next to their smart stainless-steel appliances.

To promote this business you could consider undertaking your own public relations campaign targeting various food magazines to feature your product, or you could even approach television cooking shows. You could consider promoting your product range at giftware trade fairs as well. It would be very beneficial if you could get the endorsement of a well-known chef. While it might be hard to secure a celebrity chef, you could consider targeting a well-known restaurant and speaking to the owner about endorsement.

If you decided to distribute your product range through a market stall, be sure to select a market that targets the top-end consumer, those who are happy to pay a premium for their meat and produce.

31. Promotional treats and chocolates

Many business owners seek innovative ways to promote their business to potential clients – after all, it's all about getting the attention of the customer. This business idea involves the supply of chocolates as promotional treats. Chocolates can be used by many businesses to give customers an added experience when using their product or service. Consider arriving at a B&B to find yummy handmade chocolates or other decadent treats scattered on your pillow. Alternatively, you're in a restaurant and the after-dinner coffee comes with a beautifully handcrafted treat, or you're at home when a product you've ordered is delivered with a thank-you note attached and a small bag of chocolate treats. All of the above are experiences that will help a customer not only remember their association with the business, but will help them to differentiate your service or product from your competitor's.

You could quite possibly import the treats or outsource their production and merely act as a middleman for their distribution. Or, if you have the necessary experience and skill, you could contemplate producing the treats yourself.

As a spin-off, you could brand the treats with the logo or business identity of your customers.

This business concept has great potential. The target market includes any business seeking to provide their customers with an experience that will cement their brand in the consumer's mindset. It's a lucrative idea, with opportunities to diversify into alternative markets. Initially you could target a segment of the potential market, concentrating on selling your promotional products to B&Bs and boutique hotels. From there you could expand to selling your product to reception centres or directly to couples getting married, as bonbonnieres. You might also consider targeting those businesses that specialise in selling bonbonnieres as these usually buy stock from a range of other businesses and on-sell it to the bride and groom.

You could target large conferences, those with over 1000 attendees, selling your promotional product range to the conference centre.

To market your product successfully you need to give potential customers the opportunity to sample it. There are many and varied trade exhibitions where you could promote your product. Solicitors, physiotherapists, beauticians, etc., are all likely to have similar trade exhibitions and all have clients they need to impress.

The best way to sell this product is by personally meeting with potential customers. Develop a list and start knocking on doors; it's as simple as that.

32. Knitted hats, scarves and other items

Everything old is new again. There is a growing appreciation for the skills and craftsmanship of a bygone era. As a reaction against mass production, consumers are continually looking for unique and individually handcrafted products. The number of consumers who value authenticity, style, artisan quality and uniqueness – especially in purchases for babies and children – is growing steadily.

If you are lucky enough to have learnt the old-fashioned knitting and crocheting techniques you may want to consider putting these skills to work. Using the patterns of the past you could knit your own unique and fashionable baby clothing range, including booties, hats, jumpsuits and jackets. The key to success is the incorporation of the fashionable and vibrant colours of today with the patterns and knitting techniques of the past. Ideally you are taking an age-old concept and injecting enough contemporary fashion style and flair to satisfy the consumer's demands for modern, fashionable children's clothing.

It is also important to ensure your product range is made with natural fibres. Much of the mass-produced clothing of today is made with synthetic fibres. The ideal target customer is prepared to pay a premium for clothing made of quality natural materials, such as pure wool or organic cotton.

Packaging is also another factor underpinning the success of this business. You will need to package the product in a way that promotes its individuality and handmade quality. The target market will equate the quality of the product with how it is presented.

If you haven't learnt the art of knitting, but have a flair for fashion, you could consider contracting the services of experienced knitters or crocheters. There might be mums who are willing to produce your product range on a fee-per-item basis.

The ideal distribution channel for this product is boutique baby and children's clothing retailers. Seek upmarket retailers, as these will reflect the quality of your brand. Being stocked by retailers with customers of lower disposable income will only dilute your brand and result in less profit, as you won't be able to command a high retail price from this market. You could also consider selling online, but the sites you sold through would once again need to reflect the quality of your product. A good site to check out is Mor Mor. Danish for 'grandma now', Mor Mor uses old knitting and crochet techniques to make and sell handmade quality knitwear for children up to the age of three. At Mor Mor all the employees are from the generation that made everything by hand. Their youngest employee is 68 and a grandma herself. www.mormor.nu

33. Career counsellor

It is now more important than ever that your child obtains the right advice on their future career path and the options available to them. Schools have a vast number of subjects on offer, but a poor selection of subjects could result in a limited choice of possible courses when your child applies for university.

You could be the answer to a parent's prayers by offering career advice for their children. I know I will definitely seek the advice of a professional career counsellor when it comes time for my own children to decide what subjects they will take and what impact these subjects could have on their future.

The success of this business idea is solely dependent on you and your ability to source as much information as you can about career options, courses, subjects and various schools. It will take time to develop a reputation as the guru of career advice. However, once established you will have parents lining up for your insights.

You would need to be able to provide advice on:

_ what subjects are on offer at different schools
_ what university courses are available and employment opportunities they can lead to
_ what the positives and negatives of various professions are
_ what the future prospects of various professions are – will they be a high-growth profession or are they likely to be eliminated by innovations in future technology?
_ which profession the child's personality best suits them for.

It may sound premature to match the child's personality traits at school age to a certain profession or field of expertise but personality traits don't really change over time. You are either a creative person by nature or you're not. You either enjoy exercise and the great outdoors or you don't. Personally I know if I had had better career advice when I was younger I probably would not have entered the profession of accounting. I was always a creative person by nature and enjoyed art classes at school, but my parents encouraged me to undertake business courses instead. Unfortunately, neither my parents nor I could foresee the rise of the graphic arts industry (computer design), which would definitely have been a field that I would have enjoyed working in had I known about it years ago.

To market this business you should design your own brochures detailing information about various careers, statistics and university courses. Hand these out to various schools or parents' associations. You could also design your own skills, personality and ability questionnaire to effectively assess your clientele. How successful this business is really comes down to what you make it. If you provide parents with valuable information they will rave about you. Your job is to help the client decide where their strengths are, what they are passionate about and, most of all, what path will open up the most doors for them.

To promote yourself you could consider developing a relationship with various private and public secondary schools. They may allow you to advertise your services to parents in their newsletters or magazines. You may even be able to work on a contract basis with various schools, providing consultation for parents and students.

You should also look into whether any career expos are held in your area. These could be a great opportunity to promote your services and talk directly with your target market.

Keep in mind that your prospective clients will be Internet savvy so you will need a website – one or two pages designed to get parents thinking about their child's future. You should appeal to parents by providing passionate yet realistic reasons why they should come to see you for career advice for their child.

You could also provide career counselling to adults, as there are many who dream of a new direction in life and need someone to point out what options and courses are available to them.

34. Sewing accessories online

An online sewing accessories store removes the need for a physical store. You could sell items that are easy to post, such as zips, sewing needles and cottons. Because you won't have high overheads to recover, you could sell items for considerably less, passing on the savings to your target market. To keep costs low you need to limit your product range to commonly required items that don't cost a lot to post. This is important since your target market will gravitate to your business because of the cost savings you can offer. If the cost of postage increases the purchase price until it exceeds a store's retail price then the consumer will have little incentive to purchase items from your online store.

To start this business you would need to develop a professional website. Alternatively you could use eBay to kick-start your business. If you create your own site make sure you can log in and make adjustments easily. Going back to your designer to make minor changes is usually costly.

To market your business I recommend promoting your business through various sewing clubs and associations. Offer new customers a special introductory discount. You could also use Google's AdWords to generate traffic to your site. Your site should also contain information of interest to your target market as this will help drive traffic to it. While there visitors may well make a purchase.

It is important to ensure you maximise the potential of your website to generate sales and assist with other marketing and promotional strategies. Your site should provide visitors with an opportunity to leave their contact details, such as offering free membership to a monthly newsletter. Another key to the success of this business is regular communication with your target market. Serious sewers will constantly need buttons, zips and cottons. If you regularly send out an informative newsletter with monthly specials, you will be able to generate sales from past customers. It is a lot more expensive to attract new customers than it is to continue to sell to past customers.

It is also important that your site is search engine optimised for the brand-name products you supply, as your customers are more likely to find your business through searching on the Internet for a particular product. If you can ensure your site is search engine optimised, the chances are that your business will be returned in the top ten search results. This is vitally important as potential customers do not usually go past the first page of results. Your web designer might also know of other means to ensure your business appears at the top of the list.

35. Baby holiday hire service

This business idea caters to the needs of parents taking children on holiday. If you have ever been on holiday with a child under the age of two you will appreciate exactly what an ordeal it can be. For some parents the nightmare is too great to even contemplate. You could start a business that assists parents to enjoy a seamless holiday by hiring out all the necessary items they might need while away. Common items include: pram, bottle steriliser, car seat, highchair, portable cot, bed linen, toys, DVDs, videos and bikes. You may even consider hiring various items of clothing, as sometimes parents have to buy new clothing for their child to accommodate a change in climate. I encountered this situation when I went on holiday with my children in June. We went to a part of Australia that was still very warm even though it was the middle of winter. Our hometown was very cold so the kids did not have clothes suitable for the warmer climate – they had outgrown their summer clothes some months before. I had no choice but to purchase new T-shirts and shorts for both kids, for which I paid top dollar as I was in a holiday resort area, and which they had more or less outgrown by the time the temperature warmed up in our hometown.

This business would be best operated through a website. Ideally parents embarking on a holiday could view and book the desired equipment online and have it delivered on the day of arrival. To give your customers an added extra you might want to consider providing tailored information on the various services available at their holiday destination, such as recommended babysitters and child-friendly restaurants. For parents travelling from other parts of the UK or overseas such information could prove invaluable as well as help spread news of your services by word-of-mouth. To market this service, link your website with other related websites such as international travel sites, tourist information sites and so on. You could meet with various representatives of the travel industry to see what help they could offer to promote awareness of your services. You may also wish to develop a relationship with various hotels, motels, and holiday home rental services that could recommend your business to their clients.

One of the keys to success with this business idea is the type of equipment you decide to purchase. When purchasing stock you might be tempted to purchase relatively inexpensive brands to save on start-up costs. Don't. Instead purchase well-known quality brands that are designed to last.

Parents have a price point, especially when it results in an added cost to a holiday. If you price the hire of your equipment too high you will price yourself out of the market. While the competing supplier down the road may have more basic stock they will be within the parents' budget.

Other ways to promote and market this business idea include:

1. advertising in a number of major parenting and travel magazines (including in-flight airline magazines)
2. finding out who is responsible for the publications available through travel agents and seeing if you can advertise in these

3. paying for advertising space on related websites. This way you will be able to target overseas holidaymakers as well as domestic tourists.

36. Animal breeder

If you have a love for a particular animal or household pet, you could consider extending your passion into a business by breeding and selling it. Check if you would need council approval and what laws govern this type of business. Such information could be obtained from a vet, through the Internet or by simply making a phone call to your local council. Be aware that you will also need to have an in-depth knowledge of the animal you intend to breed as your target market will look to you as the 'expert' in this field.

How you promote and market this type of business will depend entirely on the animal you choose. If you specialise in breeding a certain type of fish then you may want to consider selling these directly to aquariums and pet stores. Angelfish, for example, can fetch from £4 to £10 each in pet stores and cost only cents to breed, so these are an ideal fish to consider breeding for resale.

Develop your marketing strategy by considering where your target market would go if they wanted the pet you specialise in. Create a website and ensure it is search engine optimised so your site will be one of the first returned in a long list of results when the potential customer searches for your particular breed.

You will probably find there are various associations that attract pet owners of a specific breed. For example, the British Columbia Exotic Bird Society, www.bcexoticbirdsociety.org, in Canada was established in 1951 as a registered non-profit organisation. It provides an opportunity for people interested in exotic birds to get together and exchange information on their proper care, feeding, habits and breeding requirements. If you specialised in the breeding of exotic birds, a relationship with this type of organisation would be ideal to help promote and market your business.

Depending on the animal you breed, attending pet shows would also be an excellent way to promote awareness of your business.

37. Coffee beans

Have you noticed how coffee has become a staple part of our diets? It's big business, as you can see from the introduction of coffee franchises such as Starbucks, Gloria Jeans and Puccinos's. If you are a bit of a coffee connoisseur you could turn your good taste into cash flow by establishing a business that produces gourmet coffee beans offering a range of exciting flavours.

You could source the raw material – the coffee beans – from any major importer or wholesaler. The true flavour of the coffee is developed at the roasting stage so you will need to purchase the necessary equipment to roast the beans. Then you can sell the roasted coffee beans to various coffee shops, the general public, supermarkets and restaurants.

You will need to brand and promote your business as a superior supplier of gourmet coffee beans. The flavour of your product is therefore very important. You must ensure it is distinctive yet pleasing to the palate as this will become your unique selling proposition.

You could sell gourmet coffee beans to upmarket restaurants and cafés on the basis that your product provides a unique gourmet experience. The problem with a large number of cafés and producers of coffee beans is that their product is mass produced. Cafés and restaurants can't readily distinguish themselves from their competitors who are using the same beans. However, if the café is using a boutique blend of coffee beans not widely available in every coffee shop, that café or restaurant can effectively differentiate themselves from their competitors.

If you decided to sell your beans through an online store, you could increase the exposure and awareness of your business by product partnering with a business that supplies coffee-making equipment such as coffee plungers, filters or espresso machines. Do your research. Is there a coffee club you could affiliate yourself with?

If you think it can't be done, consider the story behind Byron Bay Coffee Company. Franco Ivancich, founder of Byron Bay Coffee Company, moved his family from Sydney for a change of lifestyle and settled in the rural town of Newrybar. In 1989 he decided to choose coffee as a way to support the family and started growing coffee trees on his land, which has rich volcanic soil. In 1997 he started to roast coffee at a friend's property in Uki, a good 40 minutes drive away. The coffee was then packaged at home and

Byron Bay Coffee Company began its retail venture into the Australian marketplace. A year later he moved into a shed on the next-door neighbour's property and purchased his first roaster, an old Greek one that had to be modified to enable Franco to roast to the style that Australians enjoy. He taught himself to roast but also had some lessons from the great Stephen Dietrich, of Dietrich Roasters fame. He began blending with international coffees and soon found he had a natural talent for it. A decision was made to remove the coffee plants on the farm and instead concentrate his energy on roasting and wholesaling. A few years later a factory was built on the Ivancich farm and a brand-new large Dietrich roaster was installed. Happy days for everyone, especially Franco who is now a very respected master roaster and blender. The proof of his talent is in the 42 awards Byron Bay Coffee Company has won for their products and the list of clients the company has all over Australia, England, Japan and the Maldives. He has now extended the factory to twice its size and business continues to grow at a very steady rate. www.byronbaycoffeeco.com.au

38. Childcare magazine

The childcare industry has simply exploded over the past five years and there has been a substantial growth in the number of childcare centres all over the world. As a parent, when you first look for a childcare facility you usually open up the Yellow Pages or consult with friends to gain their opinions and experiences of various facilities. Then it is up to you to physically visit all the possible centres to find out what they have to offer. As a mum of two I found this very frustrating. Initially I would have to make an appointment with the centre and hope the time available was not during one of the children's sleeps. Then I had to organise getting two little ones to and from the car, in and out of the childcare facility, only to discover that the centre did not suit my or my children's needs.

I found I wasted a lot of time simply looking at different centres to find one that was suitable. Most childcare centres are not on the web so I found I couldn't even check out the centre online to save time. It would be so much easier if there was a guide available to illustrate the entire range of childcare facilities, showing what's available for different age groups, what the facility looks like and the size and style of the centre. So therein lies a business idea – a comprehensive guide to the childcare centres and facilities in your region. The guide would be like a magazine and could feature advertisements promoting various related services and products, such as children's clothing, shoes or toys. Placing advertisements in the magazine would help with the costs of production. Each listing for a childcare centre would feature:

_ photos of the facility inside and out
_ a write-up about the facility, including what the centre is able to provide, for what age group
_ opening hours
_ address
_ number of spaces allocated annually for each age group
_ any other relevant information including fees and charges and staff qualifications.

To derive income from this business, you could charge the childcare centres a fee to feature in your magazine. Alternatively, you could invite the centres to participate in the magazine for free, and charge parents for the purchase of the magazine. In this situation you could distribute the magazine through news agencies using a magazine distributor.

39. Gourmet pet treats

More and more pet owners are treating their pet like a mini-me. Nothing is too good for their dog or cat. 'Doggie treats' is one of the fastest growing businesses within the pet food industry. This gives rise to an excellent business idea – gourmet doggie treats. Many pet owners are more than willing to pay a premium price to please their pooch. Making dog biscuits at home is an easy business to get off the ground as it requires little start-up capital. Pet owners are just as concerned about their pet's dietary intake as parents are about what their children eat. You could do a little research and formulate a unique recipe for healthy doggy biscuits based on natural, tasty ingredients. You could really have fun with this. Think of fun shapes and moulds to make the biscuits in. You could sell your wares to pet stores, online (eBay) or through market stalls. Even better, this type of business will really boom as word-of-mouth spreads awareness of your delicious doggy treats!

To market this business successfully, see if you can feature it in one of the many pet magazines. You might even be able to display your product range at various pet shows. You could create referral relationships with a number of pet trainers who could recommend or use your products in front of their clients.

One company to check out is Happy Yappers, which was started over fourteen years ago as the result of a tragic car accident that left front-seat passenger Milly Parker with many injuries, including life-altering trauma to the brain.

Unable to return to her studies, Milly entered a five-year legal battle for compensation at the end of which she brought a Golden Cocker Spaniel in an effort to improve her life. Besides giving Milly a great deal of comfort and confidence, Milly's new friend became the catalyst for her new business venture, Happy Yappers. She decided to use her compensation money to start a business that made biscuits for dogs. Today Happy Yappers are sold all around Australia in selected stores and online and are exported to several countries including the United Kingdom, where they are stocked by exclusive retailer Harrods. www.happyyappers.com.au

40. Quilted products

Quilted products are in high demand and they certainly sell for a pretty penny. If you have an interest in craft and quilting you could take advantage of current trends and start a quilting business. Ideally you will need to be able to quilt. However, if you can't, the good news is you can certainly learn the necessary skills through a short course or sewing classes. A range of products can be quilted: bed linen, blankets, mats, bags, table settings (placemats, napkins), cushions and wall-hangings. In fact, you could specialise in one specific area such as children's bedroom décor, creating packaged décor in themes like butterflies or fairies for girls.

Quilted products certainly sell very well through boutique baby and giftware stores. However, you could also offer to personalise your products with a child's name and sell online. You could also distribute your quilted product range through household goods, bedding and giftware stores.

This business allows you to diversify. If you have exceptional quilting skills you could start a business conducting classes and impart your skills to others keen to become quilters.

To market your quilted products successfully, I would recommend you start with a great-looking, professionally designed brochure. Then make a list of the retail outlets servicing your target market – online retailers as well as shopfronts – and send them all a copy. A week later follow up with a sales call. Consider offering stock on consignment (especially initially), as this doesn't require the retailer to invest any capital and so is often more appealing.

41. Cooking lessons

Interested in cooking? Why not consider running your own cooking classes? There are many city dwellers wanting to expand their culinary expertise or improve on their current basic cooking ability. No longer do careers and possessions serve as the only symbols of accomplishment and status. For some individuals, in order to impress their friends and work colleagues successfully, they want to wine and dine them and display their finely honed knowledge of the little luxuries of life, such as handmade biodynamic cheeses, up-and-coming winemakers and vineyards, and the intricacies of the latest cooking style.

There are a number of ways you might consider establishing a business running cooking classes. You could secure the services of a number of reputable chefs and arrange for them to conduct a series of classes. You might even be able to hold the classes at the chef's place of work, depending on the time or the day. You would be responsible for ensuring the event is organised and properly administered and you would have to pay the chefs for their time. However, if you can secure the services of chefs from well-known restaurants you will have a major drawcard for potential customers.

You could specialise in a niche market for cooking lessons, such as teaching parents how and what to cook for their babies and children. One reason why childhood obesity is on the rise is the lack of understanding about what to serve children and babies – which foods are good for them and which can do harm.

If you can find a suitable kitchen space, you could operate a dinner assembly store, teaching the participants how to properly and efficiently cook flavoursome, healthy family dinners. A business like this also appeals to consumers as it eliminates the hassle of planning and preparing meals. Businesses such as Dream Dinners do so well because the meal assembly concept offers time-starved consumers, especially working mums, an innovative and convenient way to provide their families with nutritious, tasty, home-cooked meals, with more variety, healthier options and at a lower cost than takeaway or frozen supermarket meals. By enabling customers to assemble up to twenty healthy family meals and then take the end result home to be frozen and consumed, this business idea also saves on time-consuming activities like grocery shopping, chopping and dicing, and cleaning up. www.dreamdinners.com

Of course if you have experience in the food industry you might want to consider hosting your own cooking classes. And those with extra stamina could consider cooking safaris. These involve taking a group of participants away for cooking classes – perhaps to regional areas or, for the really ambitious, internationally. To promote such a business you could contact various food magazines, in particular the more upmarket ones.

If you want to get an idea of what is already out there, simply type the terms 'cooking school' or 'cooking class' into an Internet search engine.

42. Extreme makeover classes

If you have an interest in the body beautiful or have worked in the cosmetics industry, perhaps as a beautician, you may wish to consider starting your own business specialising in women's health and beauty classes. Many young women go through their teenage years with very little understanding of personal grooming and later admit that, if they had received a few professional tips and tricks at a young age, they may well have developed the confidence to cope better with the demands of being a teenager.

This business idea focuses on hosting evening classes on a range of relevant topics, perhaps including some or all of the following:

_ how to professionally apply make-up
_ personal grooming
_ dressing for your figure and how to dress for various occasions
_ colour combinations
_ career choices
_ relationship/sex education
_ the pressures of being a teenager
_ personal security.

You could even run evening classes especially for mothers and daughters with each learning how to professionally apply make-up and how to care better for their skin. This would allow mothers and daughters to consolidate their relationship and help close the gap between the generations.

If you don't have the skills or a background of professional experience in a particular subject you could always outsource. Invite trained, fully qualified professionals to come along and speak to your members. In return they could promote their products or services.

You could run this business from one location or a number of alternative locations. For example you could host one evening at the premises of a premium-brand clothing retailer and invite a clothing consultant to come in to speak about how to dress according to your body type. Or you could hold classes at a hip café that is closed for the night so you have exclusive access.

There is a great deal you could do with this idea and a little imagination. You could possibly speak to a target group of teenagers to ascertain what issues they face in the area of personal grooming and what they would like to know so they can take better care of themselves.

To promote this style of business you could distribute flyers through a number of coffee shops within the vicinity of your business or where you intend to host your educational nights. Many teenagers frequent coffee shops soon after the school bell rings. Just remember, you need to think like a teenager in order to be able to communicate successfully with your target market. Teenagers these days are much more sophisticated. They have access to a number of sources of information, readily talk amongst themselves and are your best source of referrals. If you provide a great experience for them, word will soon spread. Look into teenage friendly technologies like Twitter, Facebook and MySpace and see how you can use them to assist with marketing.

43. Rental of office furniture and décor

Many businesses spend a small fortune setting up their offices. Yet businesses wouldn't need to make this substantial investment if they had the option to hire instead. This business opportunity centres on purchasing a range of common office equipment regularly used by businesses and leasing it out together with the option to service the equipment.

You could agree to furnish the office for a period of time –

including plants, artwork and other décor items such as fish tanks – and update equipment at the expiration of the agreement. The used furniture could form a secondary avenue of cash flow: you could sell it to second-hand dealers or through eBay. Make sure you research what equipment clients would be prepared to rent and how much they'd be prepared to pay.

To promote this business it would be important to create strong relationships with commercial estate agents because they know of clients who are on the move – potential clients who may believe it's easier to move into new, fully furnished premises than to lug their old furniture with them.

Once you have worked with one or two clients, I recommend that you take photos of the before and after results and create a brochure or even a website displaying the images in a slide show. This sales technique is especially likely to appeal to businesses that often have clients visit their premises – solicitors, accountants, dentists – and so are aware of the importance of having visually appealing offices.

44. School yearbooks

Any school could be a client with this idea! If you are a wizard in graphic design, layout and presentation you could consider designing and producing school yearbooks. The school would pay for your services to design and develop their annual school yearbook. This product would be best suited to final year students as a celebration of finishing school.

To kick-start the business you would need to organise a sales meeting with the head teacher. You may want to pitch this service as a fundraiser. To pay for your costs – your time and the costs of producing the book – you could even organise sponsorship with a number of potential advertisers, such as universities keen to get the attention of the same target market. You could approach car dealers also keen to appeal to final year students or you may wish to sign up a number of local businesses operating within the school's catchment area.

There are many websites that provide fantastic templates for creating your own book. Some sites like www.snapfish.co.uk even offer to print and produce the book as well. There is a growing trend for the creation and production of stylish personalised coffee-table books. In fact, some printers offer this service in conjunction with their usual photocopying services.

Before approaching potential schools be sure to research the costs associated with this business – you will need to know your stuff. You should be able to explain what it will cost the school and the return the school could achieve from sales of the yearbooks. If you plan to solicit advertisers you will need to know exactly what to charge to effectively recoup your costs as well as the production costs.

I would suggest you approach a school with an example of your work. Head teachers are more likely to embrace your service if they can actually see and feel the product. Once word spreads you may well find you are designing and producing student yearbooks for schools all round the country.

This business provides a great deal of scope. You could venture into producing wedding albums or documenting life stories, christenings, birthdays and so on.

45. DIY furniture and accessories

Take a dash of IKEA, mix it with a little craft and you have a business idea that involves hand-decorated kit furniture. Flat-pack furniture significantly reduces storage space when items aren't in use as well as on-costs such as freight and delivery. This idea is particularly suited to children's furniture – chests of drawers, toy boxes and bookshelves. However, you may also consider diversifying into household goods, including spice tray holders, bathroom ornaments, toilet roll holders, mirrors or bathroom stools, to name just a few possibilities.

This is an excellent idea if you are extremely artistic, creative and crafty. Value is added to the items by hand-decorating them. You could decorate the kits using paints, stencils or other decorative adhesives or accessories.

Because the furniture is in kit form, you can sell it through a website. This opens up opportunities to offer other services, such as personalizing the furniture or household goods. For example, a customer could choose a design from your range and elect to include their child's name. The child now has a special item for their room created just for them.

Kits can be purchased directly from a wholesaler or the manufacturer. Most hardware stores stock ready-made kits for a wide range of items, from tissue boxes to birdhouses. Visit the craft section of your local hardware store for ideas.

Certainly use the furniture kits sold through hardware stores for experimenting and critiquing your product range and designs. However, if you are serious about this business idea don't buy your raw materials from a hardware store. You will pay far too much for your stock and the price you will need to charge to recover your production costs plus make a profit will be too high. You will fail to appeal to the target market.

The marketing of this idea depends on the type of furniture or item you intend to decorate and resell. For this reason I shall look at a few different scenarios.

Because the product range has been hand-painted and decorated, the personal touch will justify a premium selling price. The individuality of the furniture automatically positions it as a premium product that should be aimed at the upper end of the market. Your marketing strategy should focus on this. For household goods you could target household goods stores, bedding and bathroom stores, boutique market stalls and gift shops. Some of these stores may be part of a large national retail chain. In this case I would suggest you organise a sales meeting with the purchasing agent at the respective head office.

To gain initial exposure, try to have your product range featured in some of the major home-living magazines. Contact the editors. Offer them your product range, free of charge, to be featured in the magazine. Organise some form of promotional arrangement with the magazine. You could offer to give away a certain amount of stock, provided your products are featured prominently in the magazine.

If you have decided to focus on children's products, you could market your business through various parenting magazines. Again offer a selection of your product range to be featured in the photographic product spreads. You could also appeal directly to boutique retailers of children's toys, clothing and accessories.

If you have decided to distribute your products at a market stall, be sure the stall and the market attracts your ideal target customer. It is pointless trying to sell your products to an audience who is looking for bargains and bric-a-brac. The market you decide on must reflect the high quality and premium nature of your product. You could also distribute your product range through a number of boutique B&Bs.

To increase product awareness, you could team up with a business that produces complementary products. For example, if you decorated and resold spice trays you might approach a gourmet spice supplier and propose forming a partnership where both products are sold together as a 'one-off limited offer'. Or you could have ready-to-assemble furniture with a twist. Environmentally friendly, ready-to-assemble furniture hits two trends at the same time: saving time and saving the environment.

For some examples of how this business idea could work for you, consider Jet4kids. A Dutch company, Jet4kids designs and makes furniture that is safe and stable using only child-friendly materials. Best of all, each item in the range can be assembled without glue, screws or nails, and can be put together or taken apart in less than one minute, much to the relief of any parent. www.jetsit.nl/Home-EN.html

46. Kids' parties

Many parents have been known to spend a small fortune putting together lavish birthday parties with all the trimmings for their kids. Hosting a child's birthday party is no mean feat, as any parent can confirm. There are so many things to organise. Wouldn't it be great if you could get rid of at least some part of the mammoth task by outsourcing it? There could well be an opportunity to establish a business that supplies parents with all the ingredients for a fantastic and creative celebration. The market for birthday party supplies is saturated with businesses specialising in licensed characters and TV character themes. To succeed you will therefore need to appeal to those parents who are attracted to the homely birthday party rather than the mass-market commercial themes of popular TV or film characters. You'll need to concentrate on enchanting themes inspired by fairytales, or basic wholesome themes such as pirates, cowboys, fairies or animals.

You could also consider creating your own themes. All the ingredients for the day could be neatly packed in a convenient box that was then couriered or mailed to the host – a 'party in a box'.

For example, you could consider designing and printing your own invitations, thank-you notes, decorations and stickers. You could develop games, face-painting activities, craft activities and even a shopping list and recipes for themed food. The box containing the party could be specially printed to become a keepsake that will be cherished well after the party has come and gone.

A standard box could include:

_ plates, napkins and cups_ table covers
_ helium balloons, curling ribbon and streamers in co-ordinating colours
_ birthday candles.

You might even decide to design or source costumes for themed parties. Costumes such as fairy dresses with wands and wings; Japanese kimonos; pirate hats, eye patches and cardboard swords; or paper cowboy hats and vests could all be hired out or sold as part of your service. If you were going to enter into this area, you would need to do some research to work out the most cost-effective way to produce the costumes. For example, disposable paper costumes would still need to be durable enough for kids to play in.

To succeed in this business you need to be imaginative and consider just what makes for a truly magical day in the eyes of a child and their parents. What themes will encourage imaginative play, interaction and provide educational value?

Visit the following sites for inspiration: www. birthdayinabox.com and www.favouritz.com.

47. Consulting

If your career has allowed you to specialise in a particular field, then why not consider capitalising on those skills and starting your own 'consulting service'? Generally speaking, a consultant is an advisor in a particular field who provides advice and guidance either to a business or to another individual. Since little start-up capital is required, a consulting service is a cost-effective way to start your own business.

These days it's quite the business norm to outsource special projects and tasks to those with the requisite expert knowledge and experience. It is far more practical to hire someone who has a great depth of experience than to try to manage a project with inexperienced staff or do it yourself. In some circumstances a business may need to hire a consultant to find the source of a problem. Recently a new category of consultant has emerged. These consultants specialise in assisting organisations and businesses with the transition of women into and out of maternity leave. A consultant may also be hired to support the staff, particularly if a business is under great pressure due to work commitments.

There is a host of other reasons why a consultant could be hired, far too many to list here. I suspect as times change more and more businesses will continue to outsource work because it is a more cost-effective and efficient means of successfully executing certain tasks. Businesses save on overheads and additional expenses by not having to pay benefits for consultants they hire.

To operate as a consultant you don't necessarily need a serviced office. You can set up a home office. However, you may need qualifications or to hold a licence, depending on the area in which you choose to consult. It would be highly beneficial to the initial success of your business to be able to promote significant and credible achievements in your area of expertise; for example, if you have successfully set up key systems, effectively facilitated and co-ordinated a large project, successfully tendered for large contracts, advised a board or team of employees, or assisted with the negotiation and facilitation of joint ventures, profitably managed the supply chain and so on. Such accomplishments are great examples of your ability.

To be a successful consultant you will need to understand how to network effectively and create a large group of relevant contacts that you can approach to start building up your client base. The first step is to accurately detail who is going to be willing to pay for your services and expert advice and then develop a realistic list of potential clients. Once you have identified whom you intend to pursue, consider approaching two to three potential clients to pick their brains. You need to find out where such businesses go to find help, how best to approach potential clients and what sort of sales pitch you should develop. If you find you can get a foot in the door, try speaking to the various professional associations to see if anyone is able to provide further advice and direction. In the initial start-up stages of your consultancy service you will need to 'chase the business'. You need to be committed and resourceful. It takes time and energy to build a successful consultancy service.

48. Relocation consultants

It is quite common for executives and senior employees to move temporarily from one country to another or from one state to another. For some, uprooting themselves and their families can be traumatic to say the least. A relocation consultant can make the transition so much more pleasant and minimise any adverse impact on the executive's performance. They can provide the desperately needed help to ensure the move is not met with dissatisfaction and disappointment, which can be costly for both the employee and the company.

As a relocation consultant you will need to advise and assist in every aspect of the relocation process.

The successful relocation of an employee to a new city requires the following:

_ an understanding and sympathetic approach to employees and their families at what is a very difficult time for them
_ a full appreciation of the wishes and needs of the employee and company
_ an extensive knowledge of the city and its environs and the range of accommodation types and styles available
_ an understanding of the educational system that can influence where to live and the preferred schools to attend
_ a knowledge of the lifestyle factors that will assist the employee and family to quickly assimilate into their new environment.

The role of a relocation consultant could include:

_ organising temporary accommodation
_ arranging schools
_ finding kindergartens
_ negotiating tenancy agreements
_ planning property inspections
_ assisting with service connection (electricity, phone, etc.) providing orientation and introduction to the local community.

Essentially, you need to become an expert on your region – you will need to know everything from where to locate the best beauticians to where the best restaurants are.

To market this business you will need to create relationships with the human resources department of a number of large corporations. I highly recommend putting together a strong and compelling proposal to tempt your potential clients. Ideally you want to appeal to the employer, indicating what you can do to make the transition of their staff to a new city as seamless as possible.

49. Virtual PA

Do you enjoy administrative-based tasks, or perhaps you have experience as an office assistant, office manager, executive assistant, secretary, paralegal or legal secretary? If so, perhaps becoming a virtual personal assistant is the perfect business for you.

A virtual assistant is an independent contractor providing anything from administrative support to implementation of various marketing activities. This business idea is ideal for a home-based mum, as most virtual assistants work from home. It's also a great opportunity for budding entrepreneurs who may be lacking the financial backing to start a business as, generally speaking, start-up costs are minimal and the profit potential is good.

To become successful, you need to create a solid marketing strategy and have basic office equipment – phone, computer and Internet connection.

If you wish to differentiate your business you could consider offering other services according to your skill set, such as graphic design, web design/maintenance or IT support.

To start a business as a virtual assistant you will need to:

_ decide on the services you will offer

_ determine who your ideal target customer is and how you can effectively reach them. It is smarter to focus on a particular niche; for example, one industry or profession.

_ assess the needs of your selected target market and how you can successfully satisfy them

_ create a marketing strategy. How will you appeal to your ideal customer?

_ consider what equipment you will need. What is the latest technology available to help you successfully and cost-effectively operate your business?

_ network, perhaps by joining a professional organisation or networking group. Consider which organisations will allow you direct access to your target customer.

You may find it useful to refer to the website ACS Virtual Asst Network, www.vadirectory.net. This is a networking site for virtual assistants.

A great place to start marketing your services is at one of the many virtual offices that have sprouted up around the world. Over the past five years there has been an explosion in virtual offices where businesspeople pay for a membership allowing them to use the facilities and also the office space to meet clients. It can be assumed that if a business owner is prepared to use a virtual office, they would also consider using the services of a virtual assistant. I strongly recommend that you get to know the operators of the virtual offices you approach. You could then encourage them to allow you to market your services, explaining how your service complements theirs. After all, most customers using virtual offices will be time poor and after a one-stop-shop solution.

50. Professional organiser

Are you organised? Some people are simply overwhelmed by 'stuff that needs sorting out'. A growing number of people want to simplify their lives by getting organised! Herein lies a fantastic business idea for an organised person to impart their skills and expertise to others. You could specialise in a number of niche markets: those who have too much stuff and wish to declutter; those who are looking to make more time in their lives and wish to learn the art of scheduling; or people seeking to improve their overall visual image with a more organised wardrobe. You could consider targeting mums returning to work who need to have their lives shipshape and organised in order to cope.

To market this business you could approach a number of magazines and offer to write a short article providing brief tips on how to organise your life. This exposure will help build your profile as an expert in this field. It would be a great idea to create a website. Potential customers will go to your site to read about your services. Be sure to add testimonials as this helps to create a credible profile.

Some new mums go through a major upheaval after the birth of their child. You may wish to organise visits to various mothers' groups and speak on how these new mums can get organised. Offer personal consultations at the conclusion of the meeting.

Here are a few examples of companies in the business of

organisation.

Fashion consultant Barbra Horowitz helps her clients make over their existing wardrobes, discarding dated pieces, retooling old favourites, suggesting new purchases and helping to define a personal style. Working closely with each client during an 'in-closet' session, Barbra 'edits, purges and styles' her client. She also offers advice for working with a seamstress to reinvent old pieces, selling items while they're still hot and using that money to reinvest in new fashion must-haves. www.barbrahorowitz.com

Brigitte Hinneberg, founder of Didyourememberthemilk.com, has developed a comprehensive organising system. Rich in tools and ideas, it is designed to help you better organise your household and gain greater control of your home and living situation. www.didyourememberthemilk.com.au

51. Direct selling/party plan

If you lack the capital to set up your own business, don't be discouraged.

Help is at hand. The direct selling industry has been offering opportunities to budding entrepreneurs for the past 50 years. There is a host of direct sellers to choose from. Do your research carefully and make sure they are a reputable member of any relevant governing bodies or associations.

Financial rewards are just one of the obvious benefits enjoyed by distributors; however, there are many others, such as comradeship, trips away, lifestyle, and social interaction. A New Zealand study entitled 'The Hidden Industry' found that 80 per cent of distributors surveyed felt their lifestyle had improved as a result of their involvement in the direct selling industry, and 83.5 per cent concluded they were more financially independent.

But just like anything in life you need to make a determined effort in order to succeed. The survey found that one of the key characteristics of successful distributors was their clear understanding of why they chose to carve out a career in this field. They all had a goal that motivated them to want to achieve and succeed. Running a close second was a love for the product – successful distributors are completely besotted with the products they sell.

I encourage anyone considering direct selling to examine the company's remuneration strategy. Direct selling companies differ in the manner in which they remunerate their distributors but understanding the remuneration strategy will help you to identify opportunities where you can grow your business. For example, direct selling provides one of the few opportunities to earn passive income. More often than not this is through the replenishment of product, where customers reorder product, or through the recruitment of additional distributors to create your own team and thereby earn a percentage of their sales.

Direct selling is a great way to make money while avoiding many of the troubles that plague people in business for themselves. But you do need to undertake the training a reputable direct seller will provide before you start hosting a presentation or party.

52. Furniture restoration

If you have experience in furniture restoration you might wish to consider a business that restores second-hand furniture. This business concept lends itself to two possible income streams. You could simply offer a restoration service or you could also restore second-hand furniture ready for resale. If you have skills and experience in upholstery this is a fantastic idea. If you don't have any experience in this area but are interested, there are many short courses where you would soon learn the basic skills.

If you decide to restore second-hand furniture and resell it, you will need to source the furniture to start with. Pre-loved furniture is not hard to come by. Start shopping around at second-hand stores, garage sales, charity shops or deceased estate auctions. You'll be surprised by what you find.

Select items with a solid frame that only needs a little TLC. Be very selective with the second-hand furniture you buy to restore. You don't want to get stuck with furniture that you can't re-sell even after you have totally transformed the item.

This type of business allows you to purchase your stock of second-hand furniture at a bargain basement price and add value by restoring and reupholstering it so that you can charge a much higher resale price.

Refurbished items could be sold through boutique furniture stores. Such stores are more likely to sell one-off pieces rather than mass-produced product ranges from one or two large manufacturers.

To market your business, try displaying your stock in novel and diverse venues. You may be able to display your stock in show homes and showrooms, or lend the stock to an estate agent to help sell an empty house.

To market your restoration service, you could display a before-and-after example of your talents at a local shopping centre. At the same time run a competition for 'a chance to win your own furniture restoration'. This is a great way to develop a database of potential customers. Keep the names and email addresses of entrants and follow up a month later by contacting all the members of your database to announce the winner. Include a compelling reason why the unsuccessful entrants should still consider restoring their old couch or sofa – perhaps a special consolation discount.

You could also display your before-and-after examples at home show expos. These provide fantastic exposure to thousands of potential customers.

Finally, I would highly recommend you team up with several well-known interior designers. To entice an interior designer to work with you, you may have to consider offering a special discounted price for your stock. However, rest assured that the drop in margin will certainly be compensated for by the opportunity to distribute your product through a well-known designer with a reputation and market awareness you can piggyback on.

53. Cleaning service for vacating tenants

Every month tenants move in and out of rented premises. Cleaning a rented property to make sure you get your deposit back can be a stressful and time-consuming job for many tenants. This business idea is all about offering vacating tenants an opportunity to have their property professionally cleaned, saving them valuable time and money. It also optimises their chances of getting a full refund. Services could include cleaning carpets, walls, ovens, appliances and, if necessary, touch-up painting of chipped spots or other minor repairs.

To market this business I would highly recommend you approach the property managers of various estate agents. You could ask them to recommend your services when the tenant hands in their notice to vacate. The incentive for the property manager would be that they would have a clean property available for immediate rental, as opposed to one that was off the market awaiting minor repairs or cleaning. Target popular areas in and around the city, as this is where young, time-poor professionals reside, who are more likely to use your services.

54. Laundry/ironing service

If you don't mind getting a bit hot and steamy and find ironing relaxing, this business could be for you. An ironing service saves customers valuable time and resources. You could approach a number of large blocks of units or apartment complexes and offer the residents discounted group rates. Including pick-up and delivery would make your service even more appealing. You could also specialise in using certain types of detergents and fabric softeners, from low-allergenic organic formulations to speciality scents.

Getting this idea off the ground is as much about word-of-mouth as it is about persistence and determination. It will take time for the word to spread among the friends of your clients that your services exist; however, once the secret's out you will soon find the referrals flood in.

Don't be afraid to promote your business. I recommend you try to crack the social clubs of the larger corporations. Such clubs are more likely to promote your business if you offer their members a discount. Similarly, you could appeal to potential customers through childcare centres. You would need to speak with the owner of the centre to identify the best way to communicate your marketing message to the career mums and dads who drop off their children.

Because there are low margins in a laundry and ironing service, it is wise to contain your marketing efforts to an accessible location. If you have to travel to pick up clients' clothes, you will soon find your profit margin is absorbed by travel costs.

55. Make-up artist

A make-up artist is intimately involved in the most important and exciting events of people's lives, from weddings and school formals to birthdays and other special occasions. Some make-up artists get to work with celebrities, including actors, politicians, musicians and models. Starting a business as a freelance make-up artist will provide you with the freedom and flexibility to work the hours you want. The business of a make-up artist allows you to specialise in a number of fields. You could choose to provide make-up services for actors in theatre, movies or corporate DVDs, models in magazine or advertising photographs, wedding parties, debutantes and graduation ceremonies. Or, with special training, you could help people with facial disfigurements or assist in funeral homes.

A key marketing tool to promote your business is before and after shots, as you will need to be able to demonstrate your artistic ability to potential clients. Depending on the field you decide to specialise in, you could then approach modelling agencies, theatre companies, etc., in order to source clients.

56. Personal fitness instructor

Do you enjoy exercise? If so, why not capitalise on this interest and make some money by becoming a personal fitness instructor? You could work one-on-one or with a group of clients. You will need to be in excellent physical condition to take on this business. As your customers will not only be buying your words of wisdom but also be looking to you as an expert, your appearance should speak for itself.

The recreation and fitness industry can be divided into four sectors: sport, outdoor recreation, community recreation and fitness, all of which provide services that help promote an active lifestyle. A diverse range of employment opportunities exists in the recreation and fitness industry, so people with a wide variety of interests can find suitable business opportunities to capitalise on. Health instructors don't just work in gyms, they develop and co-ordinate leisure events, from school holiday programs to sporting tournaments.

Ideally you should have some experience and education in this field. It is important to hold some form of certification. However, if you don't have any relevant qualifications, you could undertake a short course at your local adult education facility. There are also many online businesses offering training, but make sure you seek out only those who offer a recognised certificate or your qualification will be worthless.

To ensure you appeal to a wide range of customers you could consider offering a variety of services, from one-on-one consultations to hosting a stroller stride. You could even offer nutritional advice, assuming you have the knowledge and expertise to do so. You could contact retirement homes and offer a low-impact class for the residents once a week. You could even consider targeting overweight children, who may be too embarrassed or too young to use the services of a gym. I strongly recommend that you don't select just one niche market. Your success will be dependent on finding avenues through which you can grow your business.

You could conduct sessions in a variety of locations, including your local park, a home gym – either at the client's home or yours – or at various fitness centres if permitted. If you have a group you could consider using a local community hall, if appropriate. You could also develop your own fitness video to sell to your clients and to attract new customers.

To get this idea off the ground you could take on a case study, a client who would be prepared to work with you to get in shape, at no cost to them, in return for you being able to use the before and after shots in promotional material. Alternatively you could consider entering some fitness competitions, as this is an excellent way to create a profile – particularly if you win! Potential clients will have more respect for an instructor who has earned a number of awards, and you could also use them to gain media exposure.

57. Pet sitter

Some pet owners can't bear to leave their pets in a boarding kennel while they're on holiday. In fact, some pet owners are even reluctant to leave their pets at home while they're at work. In Melbourne there is now a doggy day care looking after dogs while their owners are at work – just like a childcare centre!

If you know a bit about caring for animals and have the space to do so, pet sitting could be the ideal business for you. You could even specialise in one particular type of animal – dogs, cats, birds or fish.

To market this idea, you should consider contacting pet stores and veterinary clinics within your local area. Ideally, you want these businesses to refer your services to their clients. Put together a professionally designed brochure and organise for your referrals to either hand out brochures or place them on their shop counter. It would also be very beneficial to obtain testimonials from your clients, which should then be included on any marketing material. Potential clients are likely to trust the recommendations of a fellow pet lover.

58. Dance instructor

Are you a professionally trained dancer or choreographer? You could start a business offering classes teaching people with two left feet how to dance. You will need to be a patient person with a high level of energy and creativity to accommodate the needs of your customers.

As a dance instructor you could target a number of potential customers. Couples getting married would be a good place to start. Young children wanting to learn basic steps or couples wanting to master the tango are other potential target markets. You may choose to specialise in one area of dance such as Latin American, jazz ballet or tap, depending on your particular skills.

Try promoting your business in your local community paper or community centres. You could also consider approaching retirement villages; some of the residents would be very interested in reliving their past by dancing to the songs from their heyday.

I would also get involved in community events. For example, putting on a free show at a community fair would be a great way to advertise and demonstrate your services.

If you decided to appeal to children, approach the schools in your local area and find out if they would be interested in helping you promote to their students a fun way to learn to dance. Some schools may include a promotion plug for your business in their newsletter.

59. Employee relationship consultant

Business owners today face a number of challenges; one, in particular, is the retention of staff with many business owners experiencing a high staff turnover. This can have a devastating impact on the sustainability and profitability of a business. As an employee relationship consultant you would assist a business by mediating between employees and employer and ensuring that a strong relationship is maintained between the two. You would listen to the employees' grievances and explain them to the employer, together with suggestions on ways to satisfy the employees and improve the working environment. Your aim is to ensure employees stay with their employer because they are happy, motivated and feel appreciated. This is a new, developing business concept. You have scope to make of this opportunity what you will. Ideally you would need a background in human resource management.

The best way to get this business up and running is to organize meetings with the businesses you see as your ideal target market. Make sure you have professional marketing material to leave behind at the close of your meeting. This should focus on the cost to an employer when they lose an employee, as the financial cost of not using your services is what will resonate with a potential client.

Another way to promote your business cost-effectively is to get on the speaking circuit. Look for events where the audience includes businesses in your target market, then see if you can arrange to appear as a guest speaker.

Finally, make friends with the recruitment firms. This may sound strange given that recruiters are in the business of placing staff; however, it reflects badly on them when one of the candidates they have placed resigns within the year. You could explain to the recruiter that by introducing your business to their clients you will be able to ensure the candidate's transition into their new role is seamless and that any issues are resolved before they can become a problem.

60. Fundraising consultant

Do you know a number of ways to motivate complete strangers to dig deep into their pockets to donate to a worthy cause? If so, perhaps you could start a business sharing your expertise with those institutions in need of fundraising guidance. As a fundraising consultant your clients could cover a diverse range, including primary and secondary schools, local charities and churches, volunteer groups, associations, foundations and arts organisations. Approach potential customers with a solid proposal. You will need to demonstrate your flair for fundraising and could consider volunteering your services to get some experience behind you first.

Be careful which charities you target. The bigger the charity the more bureaucracy you might have to contend with, making it difficult to get your ideas agreed to, let alone implemented. This will make it difficult to get any wins on the board, which will then reflect poorly on you. It would be a better idea to target the 'middle ground' charities: those that are not so big that they are over-run with red tape, but also not so small that they can't afford your service.

61. Promotional advertising through a voucher booklet

One of the most cost-effective means of enticing a consumer to try your product is through a voucher that discounts the price of the product or service. A consumer is much more likely to trial a product or service when there is an incentive to do so. This business idea centres on co-ordinating, producing and distributing a booklet of vouchers for a number of small businesses within a local area. Traditionally these booklets feature large well-branded stores and fast-food outlets, and are distributed nationally. Your business could offer a similar service on a smaller scale, specialising in the co-ordination and supply of voucher booklets for small- to medium-sized businesses.

This idea focuses on a niche market. Generally speaking, large promotional and direct-marketing businesses work on high volumes and can therefore offer a lower price. Small- to medium-sized businesses cannot afford the minimum volumes required by these large marketing businesses so for them this service is usually not cost-effective.

This is where you come in. A number of processes are involved to produce and market a voucher booklet successfully:

_ You will need to sell the concept to various businesses in your local area, explaining the benefits a voucher booklet can bring by attracting new customers. This may mean a lot of cold calling, but if you're a person who loves a challenge or enjoys selling, this business will suit you to a T.
_ You will need to organise the design and preparation of artwork ready for printing. If you have skills in the area of graphic design then this will be a very easy exercise to undertake, otherwise you will need to contract the services of a graphic designer to help you design the
booklet.

You may be able to use a printer who can both design and print the booklet thus reducing the number of suppliers you need to organise.

_ You will need to choose a printer.
_ Finally you need to distribute the booklets in the designated local

area.

You can often outsource distribution to a service provider such as your local post office.

To profit you need to charge the businesses featured in the voucher booklet a one-off fee. This must cover:

_ a proportion of the costs for the number of booklets produced, printed and distributed
_your cost for organising the entire production and distribution of the booklet.

Carefully select the businesses you target to appear in the booklet. You don't want a booklet full of landscape gardeners – they would not be very happy with all the competition either. To maximise the return for the businesses featured, restrict each category of business to one voucher per booklet. This will also help you to sell the concept to the business owners you are targeting, as the offer to appear in the booklet is far more inviting if the prospective client knows their business is going to be the only one of its kind featured.

The fantastic advantage of this business is that you are not bound geographically. There is nothing stopping you from contacting businesses in other regions to provide the same service as you would in your own local area. A lot of the work involved in this business is simply organising. You can outsource all the jobs required to produce, print and distribute the books. Consequently, you don't need to be situated in the state where the booklets are distributed.

Who knows, you may just create a little empire where your business is the national promotional service for small businesses! Further down the track you could consider creating franchises in each state.

62. iPod uploader

iPods have revolutionised the way we listen to and store our music. But how many people have the time to transfer their CD collections to their new iPod? Who can you call if you're short of time or don't know how to do it? Herein lies a perfect business opportunity. Why not offer a service where you are paid to convert customers' CDs to MP3 files and load these onto their iPod? Catherine Keane, in the

United States, is the founder of HungryPod, a business designed to provide just such a service. Ms Keane says she got the idea for her business from a friend of a friend who offered $500 to someone to load up her iPod. www.hungrypod.com

63. Direct selling consultant to the consultants

Have you enjoyed great success as a direct sales consultant in party plan, but are now looking for greener pastures? There are many others who would love to learn your tricks, tips and advice. You could start a business as a consultant to those who aspire to become successful direct sales consultants. There are a number of ways to generate an income from this concept:

_ You could consult one-on-one with individuals.
_ You could agree to conduct group sessions where the cost of your service would be spread among the group.
_ Finally you could contract your services to a direct selling organisation and agree to train their staff.

It would be very easy to market this business. Direct sellers advertise themselves so it wouldn't be very hard to track down potential clients. However, you would need to present clients with a compelling offer. A well-presented, professionally designed brochure will certainly help in this regard. Perhaps you could offer a guarantee with your training services.

Once word of mouth spreads about your service and the results you are achieving with your clients you will soon have new clients knocking down your door.

If you decided to approach the direct sellers, you would need to develop a proposal outlining your training program. The direct seller would want to see what they would be getting for their investment. You would also need to be able to verify your own success in the direct selling industry.

64. King-sized bows and wrap

Have you ever purchased an extra big gift for the one you love and found you couldn't find any over-sized wrapping, bows and accessories? I encountered exactly this problem when I purchased two bikes for my children last Christmas. This business idea could well fill the needs of a niche market of consumers, particularly parents who buy bigger presents for their children, whether for a birthday or Christmas, or someone who has bought an outsize gift that needs to be wrapped.

Christmas would be an excellent time to promote this business. You could consider teaming up with online gift-giving sites; perhaps for a small commission they could sell your king-sized bows as part of a customer's purchase of a king-sized gift. I strongly recommend you focus your marketing efforts on the Internet as this gives you access to a global market. Here is a site to provide you with some food for thought: www. kingsizebows.com

65. The rag trade for dolls

Well-known doll manufacturers have created a real gap in the market just waiting for a budding entrepreneur to fill. Many commercial doll manufacturers sell a range of clothing to fit their particular make or model of doll. Unfortunately these manufacturers charge a premium price for these accessories. There is a real opportunity for a creative person to make and sell their own range of fashionable clothing tailored to a number of popular dolls on the market. An ideal avenue for selling this product would be eBay. Why not piggyback on the success of the popular doll makers by giving parents an alternative to the high-priced accessories?

Once word-of-mouth spreads among parents, you would probably have to think about your own website. You could then use Google AdWords to drive traffic to your site, using popular brand names like Baby Born.

66. Family day care carer

Provided you have the space, your home meets family day care standards and you love working with children, offering your services as a family day care carer may be the business for you.

You will need to do thorough research into this idea. Depending on where you live, providing childcare services within your home may be regulated by certain laws and government standards. You may need to hold a current first-aid certificate, undergo police and working with children checks and obtain public liability insurance, and your home may need to satisfy certain safety standards. You will also need to have the necessary play and childcare equipment and will need to meet any costs associated with registration or licensing.

67. Sell your own ebooks online

They say everyone has a story to tell. Perhaps there is a budding writer within you just waiting to explode onto the net. If you have experience or expertise in a particular field, or a talent for researching, then you can write an ebook.

There is a huge market for ebooks in the United States, so be sure to tailor your book to suit an international market. Start by doing your research: find out if there are any particular informational needs people wish to satisfy. What information would an audience pay for? For older women, 55-plus, it could be 'natural remedies to help deal with menopause'; for brand-new mums, it could be 'how to organise your time with a new baby'.

Once you have found the need, you can either write the material yourself, if you have the knowledge and resources, or source your own team of experts and interview them to get the information demanded by your target market. Note, however, that some people may expect a royalty for each sale of the book, so I recommend you clarify this with your experts before you record anything. Ideally you should have a written agreement that legally releases you from any obligation to make payment. The good news is that many experts won't expect payment, as they are only too willing to share their knowledge and increase their credibility and recognition. Once you have compiled your research, it's time to write. This is where many people struggle but the best advice is to just start. When you have finished, it's time to call in what I term 'the polisher', the editor. You can access editors or even ghost writers from many online sites such as www.elance.com, www.gurus.com or www.copywritingcompany.co.uk

Once you have edited copy you have an ebook you can sell. You can sell your own range of ebooks with a simple site connected to ClickBank. This is an online retail outlet that stocks 10,000 digital products for publishers and which also has over 100,000 active affiliates who sell digital products, such as ebooks, on behalf of digital publishers. www.clickbank.com

If you would prefer to take all the glory, you can set up a

website from which customers can purchase stock directly. However, with this option you will need to spend some money ensuring your site can process payments and then allow the customer to easily download the product. Having set this up myself with my own ebooks, I can attest that it is quite difficult. Alternatively, you could bundle up your ebooks and sell customers an annual membership to all products and services. This business model would enable you to generate an ongoing revenue through subscriptions.

If you are interested in selling ebooks online, the very best book I have ever read on the subject is called *How To Make Money While You Sleep* by Brett McFall. I urge you to order a copy as Brett details everything you need to know about publishing and selling ebooks online. Another site to check out is www.ebookapprentice.com You can also sell ebooks on the site www.lulu.com

This business idea would work just as well for podcasts.

68. Sell other people's stuff

Affiliate marketing is all about turning the valuable traffic that visits your website into money. A performance-based marketing and sales solution, it enables businesses to advertise on hundreds of different websites, delivering free brand exposure until a sale is lodged or a lead has been generated.

Through affiliate programs you can sell third-party inventories on your website and get paid a commission for your services. The more products or services of your affiliate marketing partners you sell through your website, the higher your commission earnings will be. Your commission percentage will be included in the agreement you sign with your affiliate partner. Remember, not all affiliate marketing programs are lucrative online business opportunities; it is always best practice to give the agreement a through check before venturing into one.

Online marketers like www.clixgalore.com run affiliate programs on behalf of their many clients. Essentially you earn commissions on the sales you generate for the merchants who are assigned to programs offered by marketers like Clixgalore.

So how does it work? You can either create your own website or use your existing website to promote and market the clients' products. You will be provided with the necessary marketing

119

material and images, and every time someone clicks on the client's advertisement resulting in a sale you will earn a commission.

More professional marketers will assist their affiliates by providing professional marketing tools. A fantastic book that covers this entire subject in great detail is *Make a Fortune Promoting Other People's Stuff Online* by Rosalind Gardner. You may also wish to review affiliate programme directories. These are sites that contain links to various affiliate programmes. www.associateprogram.com, www.refer-it.com, www.partnerindustry.com, www.silvertap.com and Commission Junction www.cj.com , or Affiliate Marketing UK, www.affiliatemarketing.co.uk

69. Be a little crafty with your craft

If you are crafty, or have a hobby where you are able to make your own product range, why not consider setting up a shop on www.etsy.com or selling your wares on www.myehive.com? Both sites bring together buyers and sellers of all things handmade, providing the budding craft person with a cost-effective window to world markets.

However, the key to selling on this site successfully is to be unique. If you're going to command attention amongst the other online crafters, you need to be different so spend some time looking at what is already available.

To promote yourself successfully, you could consider creating a one-page website that specifically directs visitors to your Etsy site. Bear in mind that visitors land on all sorts of pages through search engines; you may well capture the attention of roaming customers who are inspired enough to make a spur-of-the-moment purchase. Create a blog and promote it on different social networks like BlogCatalog, MyBlogLog, MySpace and Friendster, and link your Etsy site to the blog. Also use Google AdWords to drive traffic to your shop and blog site. If you have craft markets in your area, don't be afraid to market yourself by handing out postcards to visitors and direct people to your online shop. It is also good business practice to network with other Etsy members who offer products different from yours.

70. Outsource your services

If your idea of cut and paste is something done via a computer program, then freelance work is an ideal option. There are sites worldwide where you can register and respond to jobs posted by other users looking for a freelancer.

Elance is a great example of a website that lets you find and hire people 'as required' worldwide. It provides an opportunity for everyone to find work specialising in what they do best. Individuals and small business owners can join Elance, create their online profile and then be immediately connected to businesses looking for their expertise. On Elance you can find work in a number of areas from web programming, design and multimedia, through to sales and marketing. As you gain work your profile builds, helping you to become a more popular candidate for future jobs. www.elance.com

Other similar sites include: www.guru.com, www. ifreelance.com or www.getafreelancer.com There are more tailored sites, such as www.getacoder.com which specialises in IT.

www.99designs.com, an Australian-based media company, is slightly different from other freelance sites. While this site still offers freelance opportunities to directly liaise with customers, 99designs is largely based on the business model of 'crowd sourcing'. This is where a customer has access to a large group of people to help produce multi results, rather than relying on a single company or freelancer. 99designs provides a vehicle for business owners to hold 'design contests' and gain access to the creative talents of the global design community. For example, a business owner looking for a new design, perhaps a logo, a website or stationery, provides a brief of their project, describing desired colours, schemes and so on. They also designate a monetary prize as well as an end date to the competition. There are no set limits the prize pool. Designers can submit as many designs as they like.

When the contest holder sees a design they like, they can award the prize to buy the design. Such competitions are a great way for even the amateur graphic designer to get online and make money, without the need for their own site. Designers from across the world can tap into a much larger market for their services, while building their portfolio, honing their skills and presenting to real clients. 99designs contests boast over 34,000 designers and more than US $100,000 is offered as prize money each month.

For those with the skills and capabilities of a graphic designer, 99designs provides a great opportunity to submit your work for consideration of the prize money. For those starting up a business, 99designs provides an optimal and cost-effective way to have your logo designed. For a relatively small investment, you can sample dozens of different design concepts from thousands of designers, thereby taking most of the risk out of procuring graphic design services.

71. Newsletter publisher

Ever wanted to take on the role of a journalist-cum-editor – telling the news as it happens? Becoming an outsourced newsletter publisher could be of interest to you.

We all know of the benefits that come from maintaining constant contact with customers. What better way than to send out electronic newsletters jam-packed with interesting and relevant information for the recipient.

A newsletter is a fantastic direct-marketing communication device. The direct mail newsletter or custom publication is a powerful tool for customer retention, brand awareness and new business development. However, there are many medium-sized businesses that just don't have the time or expertise to author, edit and design their own customized newsletter and so miss out on real opportunities to maintain contact with their customers.

You could offer your services to various businesses to undertake the production and distribution of a regular newsletter. This would involve researching and authoring relevant content for a particular business or industry. For example, if you have had experience in the financial services sector, you could contact various accountants, financial planners and financial service providers and offer to prepare their fully customised monthly newsletter, updating clients on industry laws and other relevant information. To succeed you would need to be at the forefront of industry changes and trends.

Your selling point to potential clients is the direct channel of contact you can help them maintain with their customers. After all, the key to winning business is to stay at the forefront of your customer's memory and, given that it costs twice as much to attract a new client or customer, business owners want to do all they can to engage those customers they have already attracted and serviced.

For an example of a company already providing this service, visit www.thenewslettercompany.com

72. Outsourced HR consultant

Small- to medium-sized businesses cannot afford to lose staff as they often just don't have the budget to train replacements effectively. And for many, the services of a human resources officer are also way too expensive, especially given that they probably only have enough work to occupy someone like this for three to four days a month.

These businesses often find they suffer real resource issues. If you have had training or experience in human resource management, you could offer your services on a consultation basis, providing the necessary framework to ensure these businesses have the following services:

_ appropriate remuneration schemes
_ performance appraisals
_ position descriptions
_ resolution of human resource issues
_ hiring and firing procedures
_ assisting with the appointment of new staff.

If you think there is little chance a business owner would consider outsourcing HR, think again as it's already been done in accounting. Tim Johnson started BooksOnSite in 2006 to take advantage of a gap in the market. Medium-sized businesses with a turnover greater than £300,000 ideally need an onsite accountant to manage their books better, but often only have enough work to keep an accountant occupied for a couple of days each month. Tim's company enables business owners to outsource their accounting function even if it's only for a day a month. Today Tim manages a team of 40 bookkeepers who visit clients' businesses. www.booksonsite.com.au

73. Doula

Do you think you can offer extraordinary birth support skills? Perhaps you have given birth and now have a deeper understanding of and appreciation for what women best need at this time? If so, the role of doula may suit you perfectly.

A doula, or birth attendant, is a woman who offers non-medical support and information to parents during pregnancy, childbirth and the post-natal period. The doula is knowledgeable in comfort measures such as relaxation breathing, massage and positioning, managing labour sensations using water, hot packs and aromas.

Doulas do not perform clinical tasks such as vaginal exams or foetal heart-rate monitoring. They also do not diagnose medical conditions, offer second opinions or give medical advice. Instead, a doula is skilled in supporting the birthing woman and her partner to meet the challenge of labour, one contraction at a time.

Many studies have been conducted in the United States that highlighted the huge difference a doula can make to a labour and birth. In the United States, United Kingdom and parts of Europe, doulas are a recognised part of the birthing team and post-natal services. They fill an important role, one that responds to the ever-increasing number of requests from women to have more support and continuity of care before, during and after the birth of their children.

There are a couple of things you will need to consider before taking on this role. For example, while you might only choose to do a handful of births a month, if you are a mum you will need to ensure that you can organise support and care for your own children at short notice as you never know when you will be called upon by a client.

Naturally you will also need to do a course. Some sites to check out include: www.childbirthinternational.com, www.britishdoulas.co.uk, www.doula.org.uk and www. scottishdoulanetwork.co.uk

74. Visual merchandiser

Retailers rely upon the presentation of their products to entice customers and make sales. Some smaller companies don't have the manpower or expertise to ensure their products and services are displayed in an appealing manner. You could start your own business as a visual merchandiser, offering to dress the windows of retailers. Alternatively you could approach various small business operators and offer to merchandise the stock they distribute to their retailers.

To succeed in this role you will ideally need to have experience or qualifications in merchandising as well as an eye for detail, and a professional manner and appearance.

Ideally you should take photographs of your work so that you can show potential customers how you could improve the presentation of their products and thereby increase sales.

75. Website designer

The web has become a popular way to trade. With the reduced overheads, many people now consider starting an online business as opposed to a retail outlet, so there is high demand for website designers. These days there is a host of downloadable software especially for designing websites. You can even buy customisable templates, which can cut out a great deal of the design work. One site that helps the budding web designer build fabulous sites is www.interspire.com I have successfully used this site and I'm not even a web designer.

To succeed in this business you need to have creative flair as well as a solid understanding of websites and e-marketing tools. You must also be able to listen to your clients' needs and translate them into effective operational websites. All too often designers forget the clients' demands and instead provide what they think the client should have instead of what they really need.

To market this business successfully I recommend you surf the net and find websites that could do with an overhaul. From this list of poorly designed sites, you can compile a list of potential clients to approach. Be selective: you want clients who can afford your services, so make sure you select businesses who perhaps have two to five employees or two or more branches. It would also be wise to confine your search to businesses close to where you live, as it is always better to meet with potential clients in person than approach them over the phone or via email.

76. Database management

We live in a world full of data. We have created technology that collects and amasses tonnes and tonnes of data. Sadly there is often no one at the other end of the collection process analysing what all the data means! Imagine if you were a business owner and someone offered to analyse your data and tell you where your best leads were, where sales were growing and slowing, and what the key demographics of your top customers were. You would pay good money for that vital marketing information; it would help you to tailor your marketing strategy better so your marketing spend was really working for you.

Many online businesses use e-marketing to help attract and appeal to customers. As a part of this strategy these sites secure the names and details of their customers and then continue to provide marketing material to these databases. However, many of these business owners don't have the time to ensure their databases accurately reflect current customers. You can save online businesses a tonne of money by assisting them to maintain an accurate and up-to-date database. You could even expand your services, offering to maintain the client's data and categorise the database into meaningful smaller target markets. They can then tailor their marketing campaigns and save money – even after paying your fee.

To get this business idea off the ground you would need to target online businesses, perhaps offer a contra deal to begin with: free product in exchange for a trial of your services. The idea here is to get some reputable testimonials so you can confidently show new clients what you can do for them.

77. Printing broker

Small- to medium-sized businesses generally require print material, whether it be product packaging or marketing brochures. Most don't have the time or resources to find the most economical printer and so go with the easy solution instead. You could become that easy solution, a print broker. Your role would be to take on the print jobs for clients and source the most economical quality printer for the job. In return for the referral, the printer who was awarded the job would pay a percentage of their fee to you. Once you have established a network of reliable printers you would have no trouble finding solutions for your clients.

Effectively this business idea requires you to be the middleman, acting as the go-between. Some franchises exist where, for a fee, you can buy the access rights to a well-established network of printers as well as undergo training on how to be a successful print broker.

78. Online health store

There has been a dramatic increase in health awareness and a marked trend towards maintaining a sense of inner health. You will notice a growing number of health stores in shopping centres and sections dedicated to health foods and vitamins in chemists; even the grocery stores and supermarkets now devote half a shopping aisle to health foods. Unfortunately, if you purchase health products from a physical retailer you part with a small fortune. I suspect this is because the shops have high overheads such as rent, building insurance and wages to cover through the sale of their products.

If you are interested in health and fitness you could consider establishing a business that sells health foods online. If you are a qualified naturopath, even better. One advantage with most health foods and related stock is that it is often non-perishable and has a long shelf life.

Your online health store could offer all sorts of products to assist the target market to maintain their health and fitness.

Products could include:

_ protein powders
_ vitamins
_ health foods, e.g. both organic and non-organic dried fruits and nuts, etc.

You can source your stock by visiting a health food store. Jot down the names of the major brands and contact these suppliers yourself.

Remember that before you set up an account with a potential supplier you will need to be able to prove you are a bona-fide business and have the necessary official documentation. Wholesale suppliers are reluctant to give their price lists out to the general public for obvious reasons.

To market and promote this business cost-effectively you could contact gyms in your local area. Offer a special discount on your stock exclusively for their members. You could explain to the gym owner that there is considerable benefit for their members in your offer. Passing on a discount is also a value-added extra for members and will promote customer loyalty for the gym owner. You may even strike up a long-term relationship with the gym and agree to offer regular monthly specials exclusive to their members. Most gyms communicate with their clients through e-newsletters so they could promote your product offers directly to their members.

Link your online store to as many related websites as possible – pregnancy websites and other medical websites such as the British Heart Foundation, for example.

You may want to use promotional and direct marketing services such as www.txtlocal.co.uk. Txtlocal and similar SMS marketing services operate by sending out advertising material to people who have signed up to their website. In exchange, the subscriber earns free text points, and in some cases cash, just for opening up and viewing the marketing and/or promotional material sent in an email or SMS.

79. Interior designer

Do you have a flair for decorating? Do you know how to dress a room or make the best use of a small space? Then why not leap into the area of interior design?

The role of an interior designer can range from decorating rooms with new furnishings to developing total concepts for new and existing residential and commercial interiors. Tasks can include selecting new furniture, re-upholstering existing furniture, choosing flooring, co-ordinating colours, and incorporating artwork and computer systems into workstations.

To be successful, it is important you do your market research. Do you want to target residential homes or business offices? Each will require a different approach. However, in either case you will need to identify what the unmet needs of these potential customers are in order to be able to satisfy them successfully.

80. Dog trainer

Are you a patient person? Do you have a good rapport with dogs and great people skills? Have you had success in training your own dog? Maybe you could capitalise on this success to start your own dog training school or service. You could conduct sessions in your local park or one-on-one with clients at their home. Successful dog training is as much about training the owner as it is about training the dog, so excellent communication skills will play a vital role.

People have been training dogs professionally for decades. You could take your business one step further by developing your own course that you could licence out to other budding dog trainers. In that way you would make money from your intellectual property as well as actual dog training.

If you think there is little money to be made in dog training just take a moment to consider the business empire Bark Busters. Bark Busters was founded in Australia in 1989 by renowned behaviour therapists Danny and Sylvia Wilson. Their vision was to save as many dogs as possible from being surrendered to shelters or euthanised because of behaviour problems that were seemingly impossible to solve. Since then, Bark Busters has touched the lives of over 400,000 dogs and has grown to be the largest and most trusted dog training company in the world. Trained therapists now help dogs in the UK, Australia, New Zealand, the United States, Canada, Japan, Taiwan, Israel, France and Belgium. www.barkbusters.co.uk

81. Custom sewing and alterations

For at least 75 per cent of the population, clothes never fit perfectly. The jeans are too long, the sleeves are too short or the top is too baggy. So it goes without saying that there's always demand for someone who can repair and alter clothing.

Clothing retailers in large shopping centres could all use the services of a seamstress, someone customers could bring their clothing to, to have it repaired or altered. Or you might consider opening your own alterations business. You could even offer a pick-up and drop-off service.

When it comes to altering clothing you must be experienced in removing and replacing zips, taking clothing apart only to put it back together again and knowing how to make garments larger or smaller without altering the actual form. In addition, you need to be able to hand-stitch clothing seamlessly . However, don't dismiss the idea if you don't yet have the necessary skills or experience. Plenty of courses are available, and you can get experience by offering to alter the clothing of friends and family for free.

Success in this business is largely dependent on having the right equipment. Different sewing machines perform different tasks. For example, a man's suit trousers needing to be hemmed would require a blind stitch machine that allows the garment to be sewn without stitches showing on the outside.

To market this business you should approach various retailers and offer a brochure of your rates and services. Make it as easy as possible for the retailer to use and recommend your services by providing them with cards they can hand out to potential customers. Consider advertising in your local newspaper or ask your local dry-cleaner if you can leave business cards on their counter.

To ensure word-of-mouth and repeat business add value to your work. If you're hired to lower a hemline but you notice a button is loose, fix it at no charge and let the customer know. Things like this stick in a customer's mind. Offer a 10 per cent discount to a customer if another client comes in who has been referred by them. This will get frequent customers talking to others about your work.

82. Advertising sales representative

Advertising is a cut-throat industry, probably because successful placement of an advertisement in a glossy magazine can prove very lucrative indeed. If you can sell ice to the Eskimos, then don't waste any more time: you're sitting on what could be a potential gold mine. Get to work selling advertising space on behalf of glossy magazines.

Ideally you need to have worked in the field of sales to understand and appreciate the process of cold calling, securing leads and eventually closing the sale. One of the most appealing features of this business is that most of the work is done over the phone and via email. You don't even have to get dressed for work!

First you will need to get some clients. Speak to the smaller publishers, as these are generally the ones who need the most help when it comes to selling advertising space. Arrange to be paid on a commission basis; this is usually around 20 to 25 per cent of the advertising fee.

With contracts in place, you can start selling. Most publishers will supply you with a media kit so you can gain an appreciation of what their product offers and who the target market is. This is also handy to distribute to potential clients. Then it's up to you.

83. Freelance writer

It may surprise you to learn that the nominated author of an article in a magazine may not always be responsible for actually writing the article. They may have had a freelance writer do the work for them and then paid for the publication rights. One such agency, Writing Angels, www.writingangels.co.uk, does exactly this. Keep in mind that there are also many magazines who accept or commission articles from freelancers and who do credit the writer's work.

As a freelance writer you are not restricted to magazines. Many websites are desperate for new and exciting content to hold their visitors' interest. There are also millions of e-newsletters that go out every day, the authors of which all look for fresh content to keep their readers interested. There are also several websites where you can post content for which visitors then pay a fee to purchase the rights. Check out www.associatedcontent.com or www.Helium.com.

As a freelance writer, you could also consider selling your services to publicity-hungry businesses. A sure-fire way to promote any small business is to gain the media's attention. For most small business owners this seems out of reach; however, you could offer these businesses the opportunity to either feature in an article that you will distribute to publications for print or have you ghost-write an article on their behalf. Professionals like accountants are always looking for ways of attracting new clients. Could you take advantage of this and offer a solution that could see thousands of potential new clients read their advice? There's a tremendous market for ghost-writing articles for professionals, which can then be submitted to local newspapers, trade publications and other magazines. For example, you could approach your local vet or GP and offer to write on their behalf 52 weekly articles that they or you could submit to the local newspaper. This will not only provide the business owner with excellent publicity but also increase their credibility as an expert. And as long as your rates are cheaper than traditional newspaper ads of the same size, it makes financial sense for the business owner to consider your proposal.

The best thing about this service is that it is not limited to one particular field of expertise. You could approach dentists, bankers, chiropractors, opticians, dermatologists, travel agencies or any business owner who would benefit from a weekly/monthly feature in their local paper or magazine.

A new site, www.triond.com, helps bloggers get paid for

what they do. While many bloggers just love to blog, just as many would ideally like to be financially rewarded for their time and effort. Now entrepreneurial bloggers can turn to Triond to do everything but the content creation. Triond is a simple to use and straightforward site that gives all content creators the ability to earn ad revenue for their work. Creative types write or create original articles, photos, videos and audio clips then post them to Triond. Triond distributes the content through their network of niche publishers, and content creators earn 50 per cent of ad revenue generated, paid monthly.

84. Scrapbooker

I love scrapbooking, but sadly I don't have the time to make a beautiful keepsake of all the photos I have accumulated over the years. I, like many others, would pay for someone to make a beautiful scrapbook of my precious memories.

If you are creative, you could start your own business as a professional scrapbooker. To market the business you could exhibit your talent at various shows, fêtes or markets. You could even offer classes for those who have the time but lack the talent.

85. Personal weight-loss consultant

Weight loss is becoming an issue for more and more people. There are a range of weight-loss solutions on the market, from pills to sprays to milkshake supplements; however, nothing really beats personal interaction when it comes to losing weight successfully. Some people are too embarrassed or self-conscious to join a weight-loss group, instead preferring the one-on-one consultations provided by a personal weight-loss consultant.

If you have qualifications and experience in nutrition, health and fitness or weight-loss management you could offer your services as a personal weight-loss consultant. Working one-on-one with a client provides an excellent opportunity to create a solid relationship with them, which can play a strong role in helping them to achieve their desired weight loss. And the happier your customers are, the greater the likelihood they will refer your business to family and friends.

The start-up costs for this business are minimal but you will need to spend a little on marketing. Like any new business venture, you need to spend to get your name out there. It helps if you have a case study to promote – this could even be yourself if you have suffered your own battle with weight loss. Potential customers will readily try a new service if they can see results have been achieved but no one likes to be the guinea pig.

I strongly recommend writing articles and offering these to various health magazines for free. You will be surprised how many magazines will happily print your content. It is important to build your profile as an expert and it's a great help to be able to casually mention to a potential client that you are featured in a well-known magazine.

I would also team up with various gyms to see if they would be happy to recommend your services to some of their clients. This could be a great relationship: the gym would have access to an additional service it could offer its members, without having to put you on the payroll, and you would have the opportunity to build your client base.

86. Packing and unpacking service

Ever moved house? It's not for the faint-hearted! How wonderful would it be if you could outsource to someone else the time-consuming and immensely stressful task of packing up your worldly possessions so that they arrived safe and sound at their destination?

Here is the perfect business idea for those meticulous about packing and who enjoy the challenge of clearing out a room into small boxes. You could also offer to unpack and place the customers' possessions. With a little experience you would soon become an expert on how to best set up a home.

To market this business concept, you would need to affiliate yourself with several removal companies who do not have the capacity or resources to offer a packing and unpacking service of their own. You could also consider approaching various estate agents, as anyone buying, selling or renting a home usually has belongings to pack up and move.

One company who has done very well with this business concept is Moving House, founded by Lee Hamlin and Elizabeth Yates in 1997. Hamlin and Yates left their careers in air-hostessing and small business to start the company. Their aim was to make the moving process seamless, efficient and pleasurable. Having successfully unpacked and set up homes for thousands of delighted clients throughout Australia, they now have offices nationwide. www.movinghouse.com.au. Moving Everywhere is one of the UK equivalents. www.movingeverywhere.co.uk

87. Subscriptions maintenance

Magazine publishers do a great job selling subscriptions; however, they often fail dismally when it comes to keeping up-to-date with renewals. You could offer magazine publishers a complete subscription renewals service. Using information supplied by the publisher, you would maintain an active database of subscribers set to end their subscription. Each of these subscribers would then be sent the necessary information inviting them to resubscribe. Your fee could be based on the number of renewals you secured.

I recommend that you start with self-publishers, as the corporate publishers with a stable of titles to their name will want to see you have some runs on the board before they entrust one of their revenue streams to you. Self-publishers, on the other hand, are many and make an ideal target market. Most are struggling to organise the publication of their magazine let alone worry about ensuring customers renew their subscriptions.

Before you approach a potential client I strongly urge you to consider the system and processes you intend to implement to operate this business. A potential client will want to know the ins and outs, so perhaps work-flowing the processes in a diagram would be a good tool to help support your presentation.

88. PR consultant

If you have had experience in the field of public relations and have a large network of media contacts, you could consider starting your own PR service.

You could offer two services. The first would be a basic package where you consulted with the client about what they should be doing to get their product, service or business in the media. The client would then do the hard work of pitching their business to the media. Your second package would see you responsible for not only creating the media strategy but also executing it. This means you would be the one to contact media and promote the client as a newsworthy piece. This is not as onerous as it sounds if you have the right experience and contacts. There are also online sites set up to help you appeal to the media. For example, in the UK you could use the services of www.pressbox.co.uk or www.pressport.co.uk and www. massmediadistribution.com , while www.eworldwire.com and www.24-7pressrelease.com have a global reach. Naturally you would charge two different prices for each service.

Ideally you would need to approach business owners who have had little media exposure but who have a genuine media angle. Perhaps make an introductory offer. Remember that in order for your business to experience growth you need to have a success you can boast about.

Once you do achieve the initial success, work will follow. Many business owners will seek the same level of success, so be careful about who you take onboard – taking on clients for the sake of simply having a large client base will not ensure your continued growth. You only want to take on clients that you know you can successfully promote.

This business concept will probably cost more in time to start and grow than it will in capital expense. Effectively you will be on the phone, sending emails and press releases. Your clients should pay for extra charges such as postage and the supply of samples.

89. Childbirth instructor

First-time mums-to-be often have fears and reservations about the birth process. There exists a market of women prepared to pay money to discover how they can best cope during childbirth. An alternative method, growing in popularity, is called HypnoBirthing. Whether having a hospital birth or home birth, planning a natural birth or wanting an epidural, HypnoBirthing blends the power of self-hypnosis, deep relaxation, guided imagery, visualisation, special breathing and tension- releasing techniques to help mums better manage the pain of childbirth. It has brought relief to many women and hospitals around the world now welcome this method.

You could start a business hosting courses and training mums in this method of giving birth. Of course, you'd need to receive the necessary training yourself first; visit www.hypnobirth ing.co.uk, or www.hypnobirthing.com for more information.

It should be noted that a HypnoBirther is distinct from a doula.

A doula is a companion to a woman during labour and birth, providing emotional support, physical comfort, education and advocacy. HypnoBirthing is a specific technique mums can employ when giving birth.

90. Drop shipment

Some suppliers are happy to handle both the supply and delivery of a product, which means all you need is a storefront to capture and collect orders. Drop shipment is the perfect way to set up and run an online business – you won't need to purchase stock so capital expenses are significantly reduced. You also don't run the risk of overstocking or holding obsolete stock.

The key to success is finding a reliable supplier who is happy to fulfil orders as received and deliver to individual addresses instead of as a bulk order to one location. This may take some time. However, once achieved you can start to market your business to the world. You can pay for membership to various sites that boast lists detailing the names and contact details of drop shippers across the globe; however, I have only ever come across one drop shipment list worth paying for, www.worldwidebrands.com . It is a little pricey, but it's worth the investment – other cheaper options have proven to be of little value and a great disappointment.

The success of your business will also rely on your ability to market it. I suggest you read a few good books focusing on how you can successfully market your business on the web and drive traffic to your site.

91. Wedding florist

Do you love working with flowers? Well, floristry could be an ideal business for you. The role of a wedding florist involves providing the necessary flower arrangements for a wedding, which may include bouquets, table settings, room decorations, corsages and so on. This is an excellent business for anyone with artistic flair, but you might want to complete a floral arrangement course or at least have some previous experience in the industry.

The success of this business will be dependent on your ability to design and construct beautiful, eye-catching floral arrangements. You will need a portfolio of your work to demonstrate your skills and creativity to potential clients. If you are just starting out, set aside a weekend to construct a range of unique and exquisite floral pieces. Organise to have these professionally photographed so that the lighting and camera angles make the most of your arrangements.

> You may be able to organise a contra deal with the photographer where you pay for the cost of the materials to photograph the prototypes in exchange for promoting the photographer's services to your potential clients.

To market this business, I strongly urge you to do your research and infiltrate the many wedding forums populating the Internet. Read the posts on floral arrangements. Not only will you learn about the styles and trends, but you will also gain a greater understanding of where brides go to find their florist and where you can successfully promote your business.

Consider what you can do to stand out from your competitors. Can you gain exclusive access to a certain type of flower or table setting? Could you team up with a vase designer or potter and use their creations in the table arrangements? Maybe you could include a drying service so that while the couple are on their honeymoon you could dry the bride's bouquet as a keepsake. It is important to be unique in order to encourage clients to refer your services to others. The wedding industry is referral based. Devising a creative marketing strategy will ensure your past clients continue to promote your business long after their wedding day.

Edible Blooms is one business that has managed to put a unique twist on a time-tested service. Founder Kelly Baker provides a fresh alternative to traditional flowers and gift baskets. Instead of flowers she provides her customers across Australia and New Zealand with literally 'edible blooms': arrangements of fresh fruit, home-baked biscuits and cookies. www.edibleblooms.com With this idea in mind, could the same be done for the wedding industry?

92. Second-hand books and magazines

Publishers of books and magazines face issues of overstock. It's impossible to know exactly how many copies of a book or magazine will sell so publishers are often left with some of the print run unsold. However, there exists a target market of consumers who are happy to buy an out-of-date magazine or book provided the price is right.

You could take advantage of this target market by making an offer to various publishers to buy a certain amount of their leftover stock, at a reduced rate of course. Through an online site you could then sell the books and magazines. Ideally, you should only agree to purchase a small amount of stock. Until you determine demand it is better to be safe than end up in the same predicament as the publishers.

The key to this business is keeping margins low, so I recommend you consider selling online. As most potential customers would search for a book by its title, you have a greater chance of directing traffic to your site, particularly if your site is search engine optimised for the magazine or book titles you stock.

You could consider marketing your online bookstore through book clubs, both on- and off-line. Also consider blogging about the latest titles you have read and which you happen to have in stock.

Personally I would also organise to print bookmarks with your business logo on them. If you included one of these in every order, it would be an effective and useful way to ensure your business was continually at the forefront of your customers' minds. Many customers might pass your bookmarks on to friends as a recommendation.

93. Pick-up service for eBayers

Purchasing on eBay, or eBid, is a great way to save money. However, it can be frustrating when you find the perfect item is more than a 5-mile drive away – that can be enough to put off any bargain hunter. This is why a pick-up service is such a good idea. You could offer to pick up goods on behalf of winning bidders for a set fee, based on miles travelled. For example, if the distance between postcodes is 3 miles you may decide to charge £6. You would need to ensure your prices are less than or just as competitive as those of your local postal service. Success in this business is all about co-ordinating pick-ups and deliveries to minimise your travel expenses.

You would need to advertise your services on the net to gain awareness. You could also create strong relationships with stores such as www.877isoldit.com.

One eBay pick-up service already operating in the United Kingdom is Lots2, www.lots2.co.uk

Make sure the vehicle you use is prominently decorated with your logo and advertises your service. You want to use every opportunity you can to promote awareness of your business.

94. Tourist services

If there are a few interesting things to see in the area where you live, you could start a business offering your services as a private tour guide. Do some thorough research on the places you'll be showing visitors, as you will need to have all your facts straight.

To promote this business, get the local hotels on board. You could even offer them a commission for sending customers your way.

One way to differentiate your business from other tour operators is to provide sightseeing with a twist. Instead of the usual leisurely walks around the city you could perhaps offer 'sight jogging'. This is a service already provided in Italy, www.sightjogging.it , so there's no reason not to try it in your home town.

95. Toy rental service

Instead of selling toys why not rent them out instead? Children quickly tire of toys; once they have worked out how a toy wiggles and jiggles they move on to the next whizz-bang product to hit the shelves. A child's attention span is also short so they are quickly bored. A toy rental service is the perfect solution to both problems as it means parents don't have to continually buy expensive new toys to entertain and educate their children.

The main barrier to this business idea is the initial investment required to stock your rental service. However, with a little street smarts, you can find bargains on eBay, at end-of-year sales and in second-hand outlets. You could charge a rental fee per toy or set a basic membership fee for six months or a year. To market this business cost-effectively you could offer a free month's membership to any parent who introduces a friend to the business.

To get your business up and running, I would look for ways to infiltrate mothers' groups. You might be able to place advertising materials at various childcare centres, for example. It would also be a good idea to advertise in your local newspaper. Because of postage limitations, it would be best to target mums and dads within a 10-mile radius of your base.

In the United States, businesses like www.babyplays.com have followed this concept.

96. Sell your photography

If you are handy with a digital camera and have an understanding of what makes a great photo, then why not sell your images to a photo stock library? There are several well-known online sites such as www.istockphoto.com, www.gettys.com and www. dreamstime.com. To find more simply Google the term 'photo stock library'.

You normally have to sign up and become a member of the library's community. Some photo stock libraries will ask you to submit work before they consider taking your photos. This way they can be assured they offer their customers quality images. Most will have set criteria you will need to meet and you will need to be very careful not to infringe any copyright laws.

Photo stock libraries pay per download of files supplied, so the more times someone buys your image the more money you make from it. Some photo stock libraries set specific limits; for example, when a file reaches ten downloads, it automatically moves to a new level and then sells for a higher price. For each transaction the photographer receives a percentage of the fee. Most stock libraries will make payment once your account reaches a set balance.

If you are looking for greater control in selling your photography, look no further than www.fotomoto.com. This is an e-commerce system specifically designed for photos that enables photographers to sell images on their own website rather than sending potential customers to a photo supermarket. If you are a photographer or you operate a website with a big photo inventory, Fotomoto can help you to monetise your photos and sell them in a professional way on your own site. Best of all, Fotomoto takes care of everything from processing orders and payments, making prints (or other products based on your photographs), and shipping the orders to the customers on your behalf. Their goal is to let photographers and content owners focus on their photography without worrying about the hassles of selling.

97. Sell your artwork

If you are an artist you could consider selling your artwork to the world through RedBubble www.redbubble.co.uk. This is an open and inclusive website where you can share your creative genius with the world and sell your work online. Over the last nineteen months RedBubble has shipped 114,000 items of art to 71 different countries. All you need to do is to provide your digital file and RedBubble will turn it into the finished product, deliver it to the customer and take care of any customer service problems.

Similar to RedBubble, Café Press, www.cafepress.co.uk, can turn your digital file into a framed print, poster, canvas print, T-shirt, greeting card or your very own calendar that you can sell from its site, eliminating the need for you to have your own merchant facilities. You control the pricing of your work – neither site charges a commission; instead they have a simple base-price framework. While these two businesses can certainly manage supply, you will still need to consider how you will appeal to your target market and build awareness of your product range. How you go about this will be entirely dependent on the target market you are trying to appeal to.

98. Expense reduction

Do you have an eye for detail and know how to spot an unnecessary expense? Then you're just the asset many businesses are looking for. A cost cutter is someone responsible for reviewing the expenses of a business to find where and how it can reduce its costs. This business concept has great appeal: the mere fact that you can find where and how to cut expenses more than justifies your appointment to potential clients. You will, however, need to have demonstrable experience and expertise in this area.

To kick-start this business it would be a good idea to consider public speaking opportunities at events attended by your target market. These will help to raise your profile and create awareness of the benefits your business can offer. You'll also need to rely on cold calling to build your business, but once you have a few satisfied clients, word of mouth will ensure a steady stream of new ones. It's surprising how testimonials can enhance the reputation of your business and help it to grow.

Ideally, you should structure your business so that you are paid a percentage of the costs you are able to cut. Few business owners will readily take your services onboard if you ask to be paid by the hour; they like to be reassured they are getting value for money.

One business in the United Kingdom that is already cutting the costs is www.costcuttingservice.co.uk

99. Rent a pet

Sadly, come Christmas time, many families adopt a pet only to realise it involves more than they bargained for. Hindsight is a wonderful thing, and now you can provide this with a business that rents out pets. Instead of going through the harrowing process of picking out a pet and then realising it isn't quite what they expected, clients can have a trial run to see how it goes first.

Certain pets make ideal rentals: dogs, caged birds, cats, rabbits and hens. If you have enough land to house a collection of these animals you could offer them up to families to try before they buy. You could also work together with a breeder: once the customer has agreed to take on the pet they organise the purchase of that particular breed through the breeder.

To market this business you will need to appeal to parents unsure of whether they should go down the path of pet ownership or not. It's a 'try before you buy' opportunity, making it much easier for parents to deal with things if it turns out the pet doesn't fit in with the family or the children aren't yet up to the responsibility of caring for an animal. It would be a good idea to promote your business to the media as 'a saviour, helping to reduce the number of abandoned pets'. Now that's wonderful free advertising!

Two businesses in the United States already renting out pets are www.strayrescue.org and www.flexpetz.com. In Australia, you can rent chickens at www.rentachook.com.au

100. Pet photography

Love animals and photography? Why not combine your interests and make some money. Pet photography is fun and rewarding. Owners of dogs, cats, reptiles, horses, birds and particularly show animals are all potential customers. Best of all this business can be operated from a home-based or mobile studio. To make your pictures interesting and fun, use a mixture of natural surroundings, toys and backdrops. I recommend you offer a framing service too, as this way you can charge a little extra and also ensure the pictures you provide look fantastic. Framed pictures always look better than prints.

It is also a good idea to offer a wide range of photographic products such as key rings, mugs and T-shirts. It's incredible how many pet owners cherish these added extras. Many see their pets as part of the family and are willing to spend as if they were purchasing irreplaceable images of their own children.

To be successful, make sure the experience you provide is fun for both the pets and their owners as this will help encourage referrals. It's therefore important that you have a great rapport with animals.

To market your business, you might like to build relationships with your local pet shop or vet. Ideally you want these businesses to recommend your services. You could also organise to appear at various pet meets, like dog shows, where pet owners are proudly showing off their pets and would be more than happy to pay for their picture.

101. Dog clothing and accessories

You can earn money by designing, making and selling designer clothing for dogs. Doggie 'jumpers' and 'rain jackets' are obvious items. Less is best: don't try to over-design a garment with all the bells and whistles. Do a little research and find out what's already available, what's working and what's not. Look for where you could make improvements to current designs. Personalise your range by giving each style of garment a name that a pet owner could easily identify with.

You could sell your designer range online, through a vet's office or pet shop, or at various pet shows and competitions.

You will need some level of sewing skill; however, you can learn these skills by taking a course. Fabrics are key as the garment you produce must satisfy the dog owner's needs while making the dog both feel and look good. Ensure your clothing is clearly branded so that dog owners can easily identify who made the garment and where they can purchase items online.

102. Technology training

Each year technology gets more and more sophisticated and, unless you're a 'tech head', it can be hard to keep up. The younger generation are far more tech savvy, while the older ones are scratching their heads, which leaves the budding technical entrepreneur with a market of customers willing, ready and mostly able to learn the ins and outs of new software. Whether it's the features of the latest mobile phone, a new camera or software to enhance and modify digital images, you can bet there are people desperate to learn how they can increase their technical comprehension of a product.

With advances in technology you can now host tutorials virtually. Using a simple website, web video or teleconferencing, you could be teaching anyone from anywhere around the world.

An ideal target market to appeal to would be retirees and/or baby boomers. You could consider marketing your services to retirement homes, offering a five-week workshop of one-hour tutorials on a specific type of technology, such as a digital camera. Many baby boomers have grandchildren who are well versed in new technology so an additional marketing angle would be how the course could empower your clients to be able to communicate effectively with younger family members.

You could also approach camera stores and mobile phone retailers and sell your services as an add-on for customers who purchase such products, irrespective of their demographic. You could offer a set-price, one-hour tutorial on how best to use a specific type or brand of camera or telephone. If you are savvy you could organise for the retailer to pay for the service and incorporate it into the overall purchase cost, using your course as a selling tool to motivate customers to buy that particular phone or camera.

Alternatively, you could tap into the younger generation, who are keen to stay abreast of the latest and greatest gadgets and gizmos. You will need to be creative in how you reach this target market, however. Consider where members of this generation shop and how they communicate with each other. It may well be that online tutorials are the way to go in this instance.

103. Errand runner

Ever wished you had someone you could turn to, to run those everyday, time-consuming errands? We all have, at one time or another, wished there was someone who could take over everyday tasks such as:

_ picking up the dry cleaning
_ stopping by the supermarket to pick up one or two essentials
_ walking the dog
_ dropping the car off for a check-up
_ organising travel and other engagements
_ ringing around for quotes.

Given the ageing and time-poor population, errand runners are becoming increasingly popular. If you don't mind doing the running about for someone else, this could be the business for you. You could extend your services and offer to run errands for concierges at upscale hotels. To be successful, you will need to be organised and have great people skills. If you lack effective time-management skills you will probably struggle.

Errand runners can charge by the hour or use a flat fee system; it really depends on what the market will bear. The range is £6 to £30 per hour, including travel time. With the price of petrol increasing, be sure to factor the cost of travel into your charges.

To get your name out there, you might consider having a professional brochure designed, detailing who you are and what you do. Leave this where members of your target market will frequent; for example, you could ask your local dry-cleaner if you could leave your brochures on their counter.

Suburbs where professionals and the wealthy live are also great to target, but middle-class suburbia may not be able to afford your services irrespective of whether they need your help or not.

You might want to contact the human resources department of large corporations as some of these businesses offer executives a concierge service as a perk and might even have a corporate concierge on the staff with whom you could team up to share the work.

Also consider retirement villages. Older people with mobility problems might welcome having someone available to walk the dog or run other errands for them.

104. Bereavement services
When a friend, colleague or family member experiences a bereavement, it can be difficult to find the right words of comfort or the right gift for them. There are opportunities in the market for

online businesses that stock gifts suitable for those mourning the loss of a loved one. A bereavement gift is a step above flowers and shows a lot more care and thought. It's a keepsake that will last forever.

A few businesses around the world are already offering this service. Consider, for example, www.bereavementstore.com, www.acknowledgements.net or www.shirleyfamilygifts. com.

I would highly recommend also marketing this business idea online, as the target market is likely to turn to the Internet for guidance when searching for an appropriate gift. You will, of course, need to ensure that all promotion is tasteful.

105. Rent a tie

Looking for a business idea for a home-based business that taps into your great fashion sense? My husband spends upwards of £40 on a tie and he updates his collection about ten times a year. This sounds like a lot but when you consider the only option a man has to update or refresh his suit is through a new tie, it doesn't seem that bad. Nevertheless £400 a year for a few small pieces of fabric that will eventually date is crazy. It would be wonderful if there was a service that allowed him to hire his ties for a small monthly membership fee.

Nowadays we hire designer handbags from www. handbaghirehq.co.uk or www.frombagstoriches.com and a host of household items from sites like www.rentoid.com.au. However, I am yet to find a site that hires out products like designer ties and cuff links, so there's a market crying out to be tapped.

Men are more fashion conscious than ever before; the explosion of men's magazines is testament to this. There exists a real market of fashionista men who would willing pay a monthly membership fee to hire a month's supply of ties so they can look good.

Ideally this is an online business, providing professional businessmen with direct access to order online. It would need to be an easy and seamless experience for the client. Within a day or two the customer would have their month's worth of ties shipped directly to them. Supplying prepaid bags would allow members to easily return the ties at the end of the month.

The membership fee should include the cost of dry-cleaning, postage and handling. There would be an initial investment in ties and cuff links, but this should be recouped as a proportion of the membership fee. You would need a website that was tailored to your business model. It goes without saying that you couldn't have ten customers order a tie if you only had five in stock, so your site would need to be interactive to ensure customer orders were based on real-time information on stock levels.

To ensure you covered all your costs, it would be wise to make customers pay for a minimum three-month membership, which they would need to exercise in consecutive months.

The membership could also cover different levels: standard membership would cover basic ties, whereas premium membership would include expensive designer ties and be geared towards men who were more meticulous with their presentation. Membership would make a great gift idea for any man who had to wear ties often.

106. Resell a bargain

We all know eBay is an excellent place to buy things no longer needed. Sadly, many budding eBayers sell their unwanted goods for way below market value, purely because they haven't marketed their sales well. By reading a book or two on how to maximise your selling potential on eBay as well as perhaps taking a course offered by a reputable provider, you can learn how to sell on eBay successfully. Buy up great bargains and then instantly resell them. Your profit is the difference between what you pay for the item and what you are able to sell the item for yourself. The advantages of this business are no stock and very little capital investment!

There are three fundamental mistakes that people make which result in a failure to command the market value of their item. The first is not providing a great picture. People do not like bidding on what they can't see. With a digital camera in hand and a better understanding of how to take an appealing product photograph, you can overcome this problem. When you're buying, find auctions without photographs using these search terms: 'email me for photo', 'sorry no photo' or 'sorry no pic'. You will be surprised how many people list on eBay without including a photo of the item. This is where you can grab a bargain. If there are no bidders, that's great! It means a lower purchase price for you and a greater chance of a higher selling price.

The second mistake is setting the auction to end in the middle of the night. Most people don't want to stay up all night just to get in the last bid. However, if you are willing to burn the midnight oil you will more than likely be the last person to place a bid and probably bag a bargain in the process. Since most bidding occurs on items at the end of an auction, this effectively means that there is zero competition on these items, since everyone is asleep, and they can often be had for way below market value. To find these auctions, sort your search results according to ending time and then target auctions ending after 1 a.m.

The third mistake that you can capitalise on – but should not repeat yourself – is misspelled listings. You can get some great deals at auctions where people have misspelled the name of the item, causing it to remain hidden from people who are searching for it using the correct spelling. Most eBay buyers search on brand and model names when looking to buy. If you want to bag a bargain for resale, make sure to search using as many incorrect spellings as you can.

107. Home theatre installation

Welcome to the digital age: we have more gadgets and gizmos than we know what to do with. Worst of all, for most of us it's a feat just to connect up the latest innovations and get them to work. If you are savvy with instruction manuals and have a knack for electronics you might enjoy running a service business that installs and sets up home theatres. An excellent way to source new clientele is to ask your local audio-visual equipment stores (if they don't already provide an installation service) to recommend you to their clients for a percentage or fixed fee. Many people will gladly pay £30 or more for a couple of hours of high-tech handholding.

108. Selling bulbs

There is good money to be made from selling flowers that come from a bulb. Better yet is to sell the bulbs of flowers like tulips. These plants actually multiply all by themselves. You plant the bulb in winter, the plant flowers in early spring and summer and then it multiplies in the ground just below the surface. Even though you started with only one bulb, by the end you can find you have four.

Then you dig them up, separate them and sell them. That's four bulbs for resale and you haven't done a thing! You could sell these at the local markets, nurseries or online (although you would need to check the postal regulations). Find other bulbs that multiply and you will certainly multiply your ability to make money.

109. Catering

If you are a bit of a wiz in the kitchen, perhaps a catering business is for you. This is an excellent way to generate an income. Orders are usually placed in advance, which is an advantage as you are able to pre-order ingredients and purchase the necessary stock to make up the orders.

The success of this business relies on a combination of two factors:

1. You need to be able to deliver high-quality tasty food.
2. You need to deliver first-class service.

Once the event has come and gone the two main things the event organiser will remember are how the food tasted and, most importantly, the ease with which the food was ordered, prepared and delivered. If you make it hard for the customer to order or for guests to eat the food, or fail to present the food in an appealing manner, it will be remembered. You need to be able to give your clients an experience above and beyond that of your competitors so the client will remember you positively and talk about you with great enthusiasm. That way you will get the call-back for their next function as well as referrals.

You need to ensure you can legally run a catering business from home. It would be wise to read up on food preparation and handling regulations and obtain advice from your local council. Even if your home kitchen does not meet the food-handling standards required, it might be possible for you to hire a commercial kitchen for a few hours a night, maybe one or two nights a week – perhaps a café that is closed after 5 p.m. would be interested in hiring out their facilities. You would need to have proper storage facilities at home and these would also need to meet the health standards and regulations.

The overall target market for a catering business can be segmented into smaller groups with similar needs. You might consider specifically targeting a smaller group of potential clients as you establish your business. For example, you might consider targeting small businesses in your local area. There are many businesses that regularly call upon the services of a caterer to provide lunch or light dinners.

Finally, another niche market you may want to consider servicing is the 'in-house' catering service. Here, the caterer goes to the client's home where the function is being held. They are responsible for preparing the food, which may involve assembling a smorgasbord from which the guests can help themselves or acting as an in-house chef cooking meals for a dinner party. The caterer is required to source the necessary ingredients and, in some cases, the cooking appliances. This form of catering is becoming very fashionable. It saves the host from having to run around preparing food all night and the food is served hot and fresh.

110. Home stylist

With the slowing down of the property market, vendors need to do all they can to market their home if they want a great sale price. This creates a business opportunity for a home stylist, who can help a seller get the best price by identifying how to arrange existing furniture and knickknacks to hide the property's less appealing features. The stylist's role is really to make the home as attractive as possible to prospective buyers. If the house is vacant, the home stylist can even rent furniture and other accessories to show off its potential. You can easily advertise your services to estate agents and in property magazines. If you have a knack for decorating and an eye for design, this can be a fun business to start.

Begin by approaching your local estate agents. If they can sell a house for a higher price, they receive a larger commission, meaning that it's worth it to them to refer you to clients. Make sure you take before and after shots and keep documented evidence of the assessed value of the home before and after your service, including what it sold for. This information is incredibly valuable in selling your services to new clients.

And if you think people are not prepared to pay for this service, think again! Check out the following sites for some inspiration: www.housewow.co.uk, www.houseweb.co.uk, and www.homestagers.co.uk

111. Rent a box

When moving house you soon find you have a seemingly endless need for strong cardboard boxes. This is why hiring out cardboard/moving boxes is a great business opportunity. You could organise to have your own made or start to collect large boxes from various retailers. To market this business you could approach companies who hire out trucks and vans for the purpose of moving. Often these businesses do not rent out boxes, so you could strike an arrangement with the truck company to pay them a commission for every client who also books the hire of boxes.

112. Thank-you notes

So much preparation goes into planning a wedding; however, after the big day is over and the fun has been had, there are still a lot of loose ends to tie up. Sending thank-you cards is often the last thing on the just married couple's mind. But it must be done. So why not offer this service? As a professional wedding thank-you note writer you can alleviate the burden of this time-consuming but necessary task.

Get the word out about your services through wedding planners and other businesses in the wedding industry. If you have systems set up so that the gift and the sender are recorded when the gift arrives, you will find this a very easy business indeed. You should be able to earn at least £1 per thank-you plus postage for your notes. As some guest lists run into the hundreds this could work out to be a nice little earner indeed.

113. An assembler

These days most furniture comes flat-packed. If you're good at putting things together, you can make money helping people with their ready-to-assemble furniture. There are many young women, singles and the elderly who would find it difficult to put together a large storage unit, for example. To promote this business you could speak to one of the largest flat-pack furniture suppliers, IKEA, and see if you could leave your cards at their checkout counters. You could also promote your business through home-style magazines. There is little capital investment required since most flat-pack furniture sets come with clear instructions and allen keys to go with them. All you'd need are a couple of screwdrivers and a mallet, and you're in business. You could charge an hourly rate or a flat fee.

114. Advertising consultant

Where do you go when you need to locate a service? The Yellow Pages? Or do you look to advertising? Sadly many small-business owners waste thousands of pounds on advertising, making outrageous claims or communicating the wrong message. But as they lack the budget for an ad agency, they have nowhere to turn for help. You could be their saviour, teaching them how to make the most of their advertising.

If you have no idea about advertising don't stress. Though you do need a keen interest in marketing, you can learn all you need to know in several books by Brad Sugars. Other gurus in all things related to advertising and marketing are Mary Portas and Lynne Franks; check out their websites at www.maryportas.com and www.lynnefranks.co.uk

To pinpoint your ideal clients, simply open up the Yellow Pages and start looking for the ads that just don't work. You will soon spot them.

Once you can show a business owner that you can bring in more customers without spending any more money, they'll gladly pay you and refer your services.

115. Dog Day Care

Conscientious dog owners really don't like the idea of leaving their pet alone in the backyard all day, and apartment owners don't even have that option. So it's not surprising that there are thousands of people willing to pay for someone to look after their dogs while they're at work. What could be easier than starting a dog day care service? With a few advertisements, you should be able to attract enough dogs to occupy your day. You could even go one step further and offer to feed the dogs a homemade meal; after all, what doting pet owner wouldn't want that luxury five-star treatment for their pooch?

You could advertise through your local vet or see if you could get access to the social clubs of some large corporate offices – those based in the city would be ideal – and offer an introductory rate.

116. Logo designer

Large corporations pay hundreds of thousands of pounds to graphic designers to design the logo that will represent their company. It's big business. But for the smaller business owner this service is just not within reach. This is where you could help, by setting up a business specialising in affordable logo design. All you need is graphic design software like Adobe PhotoShop® or Illustrator® and you're on your way. With technology on your side, you could be designing logos for thousands of businesses around the world. Appeal to potential customers by partnering with web design businesses that offer 'start-up services' such as an accountant to register the business owner's company.

117. Freelance gym instructor

What do gyms do when their instructors take a sick day? Where can they find replacements at the last minute or someone to fill the gap as and when required? If you are a trained fitness instructor, perhaps specialising in aerobics, yoga or Pilates, you could consider outsourcing your services. Why stick with one gym and receive a standard wage when you can work your own hours where you want and charge what you want?

Best of all, very little start-up capital is required. You simply need to have the necessary qualifications and then make yourself known to the gyms in your local community.

118. Jammed up

Homemade jams, relishes and spreads will never lose their homely appeal. With the growing popularity of boutique gourmet food stores, there is an ever-increasing demand for this style of product based on traditional 'homemade' recipes. You could experiment with various recipes and ingredients to develop a unique and deliciously tasty range of jams and spreads.

To appeal successfully to the target market for homemade jams and spreads consider how you could innovatively package the product. There are many packaging suppliers who could provide some imaginative suggestions. Steer clear of quirky and overly commercial styles of packaging. Take a look at what is currently stocked at popular food stores in your local area. This will help you appreciate the packaging style of your competitors. You may also wish to purchase copies of current 'foodie' magazines such as *Good Food, Foodies Magazine* and *Bon Appétit*. Are any potential competitors advertising or featured in these magazines? If so, consider their approach. Can you identify ways you could better the competition?

This is another excellent example of a business that is not limited by the selection of a distribution channel. You could sell directly to cafés and restaurants, and if you package your product in smaller containers you could consider selling these to B&Bs or any other type of accommodation facility that offers breakfast. Finally you could appeal to your local market by distributing through community market stalls.

It is important to develop a thorough understanding of all the applicable health regulations and council permits to ensure you comply with the laws governing food preparation and handling.

By the way, if you think there is no money or long-term future in jam just visit Fraser Doherty's site: www.superjam.co.uk. At the tender age of fourteen, Doherty was bubbling up vats of jam from his grandmother's recipe book, which he would sell to friends and neighbours after school. Within four years he was producing up to 1000 jars a week from his parents' home in an Edinburgh suburb. In 2007 he started supplying Waitrose and now his SuperJam is available in over 1000 outlets across the United Kingdom. He has now moved into a small factory to cope with the growing needs of his business.

119. Removing unwanted rubbish

For most urban residents getting rid of rubbish such as broken TVs, old computers and general junk is hard. Your local council usually allocates a handful of days each year where they will pick up your junk for free, but what if you are moving house or have simply bought new furniture? There's a need for a man with a van, so to speak. With a partner you could hire a small truck and be paid to pick up junk. To appeal to customers you could promote your services through a mail drop, focusing on one suburb at a time, or through estate agents that continually see people come and go. Payment is made prior to pick-up, so you would need to tell your customers to be home or organise advance payment. The customer then leaves their unwanted goods on the roadside or other suitable place for pick up. Once the business proves its worth you could consider purchasing a truck. In the meantime hiring a truck would reduce the capital investment required to get this idea up and running.

120. Customised ceramics

Are you into ceramics? If so, you could have a nice sideline business that creates custom tile murals for people. Custom tile murals are extremely popular in new home constructions – in bathrooms, kitchens and gardens many of the well-off look for unique features to give their home the 'Vogue appeal'. This idea works just as well for those who are into mosaics.

If you are going to focus on garden feature walls or paths you could promote your business through nurseries. For feature walls in the bathroom and kitchen you could consider approaching various kitchenware and bathroom outlets that sell taps, basins and so on.

Perhaps you could even create a spectacular wall in your own home and submit photos of it to fashionable home-style magazines. You never know, they might run a story on your business – instant advertising!

121. Sell sports memorabilia

Sports fanatics are everywhere! You can make money from this passion by selling on eBay memorabilia signed by famous sportspeople. Note that something signed by several players is always worth more than an item signed by only one person. Look out for events where there are many celebrity sportspersons, then attend armed with a pen and the item you want signed. Be careful how you approach the players. It's probably not a good idea to let them know you are going to sell the item for profit, but you certainly shouldn't lie and say it's for a charity either. Consider having the item professionally framed to further increase its value.

eBay is an ideal way to kick-start this business, as many potential customers will search for memorabilia based on their idol's name. eBay also provides a cost-effective vehicle for selling the memorabilia. As your business begins to grow, you can consider starting your own site.

122. Staining

Depending on where you live, the summer sun can be harsh, drying out your timber garden furniture and decking. You don't realise the effect until next year, when summer rolls around again and you start to spend more time outside. Every year wooden decks and garden furniture should be stained if they are to remain in good condition. You could take advantage of this and offer a staining/oiling service to local home owners. It takes no time at all to apply a protective coating and the home owner sees the improvement straight away, making them happy to pay your fee. For jobs requiring a little more professional care, perhaps because there has been a lack of attention for several years, you could charge more.

To promote this business try a letter drop. Make sure you include before and after shots in your advertising so the home owner can see what a great job you do.

Alternatively you could affiliate yourself with your local hardware stores and ask them to recommend your services to customers purchasing stains and protective finishes. You could offer a discount on your services to customers who have already purchased the raw materials.

123. DVD burner

DVD has well and truly replaced video. But how many of us have hours of footage on outdated videotape? Eventually there will come a time when we won't be able to view these precious memories because the technology will no longer exist. You can capitalise on this by offering to transfer images on videotape to DVD discs. There is a huge market for this service. Just think of all the home videos out there! You will need to invest in the technology to convert videotape to DVD; however, the financial outlay is minimal and you will have made your money back after only a few clients.

Pass out fliers to market your services at school and church functions, or place ads in the newspaper. I would also recommend you promote your services through video rental stores. The chances are that many of their customers will have videotapes of special family events that they would love to have converted to DVD.

124. Promote your local community

People move between regions and to new suburbs on a daily basis yet there is no welcoming party to introduce the new resident to the local services. You could provide this service through estate agents or the council, and for a fee promote businesses in your local community. Local companies would pay to have their products (or coupons for their products/services) included in a special 'welcome basket' for new arrivals to an area. A new resident does not have any established loyalties so it's a great opportunity for a local business to get in first. Chances are the new resident will be more likely to patronise the businesses that welcomed them with a free sample or discount. In addition to the coupon or sample, each business would pay you £30 to £60 a month to supply them with new customers. In some areas, you could get 100 businesses to participate in this manner, each paying you £30 (or more) a month to introduce their product or service to new residents. It might take some time to build up a business this way, but if you were the only one doing it in your area it would probably be fairly easy. Once you worked out the winning formula there would be nothing to stop you implementing the same business idea in other communities.

125. Make music and sell it

If you're musically inclined and if you've got a keyboard synthesiser or a computer and associated music software, you can start a business creating royalty-free ambient music. Radio stations, television stations, video editing companies, ad agencies, production studios, etc., are always buying CDs of royalty-free music that they can use in their productions. You could even sell your tunes to businesses such as naturopaths, beauty salons, massage therapists – the list is endless. And since your customers won't want to use the same old music all the time, they'll buy new

CDs on a regular basis.

With modern synthesisers, it's possible to create interesting sounds and mood music with very little effort. The best way to market the CDs would be to set up a website with retail capability, and then optimise your website so that it appears on search engines when people search for 'royalty-free music'. This would also enable you to set up a facility for customers to download your music as MP3 files.

To start selling your tunes, you should consider sending samples to your ideal target customers, along with a brochure setting out your product range and price list. Initially you may find you send out more samples than you receive in sales, but understand that it takes time to build a business.

126. Buy and sell native art

If you have the right connections, you could capitalise on these relationships and go into partnership selling native art. Indigenous art from Australasia and Africa, for example, is incredibly popular and the Internet now makes it much easier to source stock. All you have to do is get a few good contacts where you can buy nice pieces directly from the source. Note you will need to check with Customs to ensure you do not violate any import or export rules. You would also need to be aware of any tribal or indigenous customs and traditions with respect to the artworks. You could set up a website to sell your stock of art.

127. Proofreader

Do you have an eye for detail and enjoy reading? Perhaps you could consider a business as a freelance proofreader. One of the advantages of this business is that you will have an ample supply of reading material! I would recommend taking a course from an accredited provider so that you have a certificate to verify your skills.

To get started, you could consider approaching various publishers and offering your services, perhaps on a contract basis. Alternatively get your name out and about in the literary community; you will be surprised by how quickly word will spread. You could also sign up to various freelance websites and offer your services worldwide. Visit www.guru.com or www.

freelance.com. Writers' centres are another possible source of work, as are web designers. Wherever there is copy to be proofed, there's a need for proofreaders! Record your customers' testimonials as these will help you to secure future business.

128. Ceramics

Ceramic work lends itself to household items such as plant pots, picture frames, plates, vases, decorative tiles and ornaments. If you have creative flair then this may well be the business for you.

One of the best features of this business is that you can either make or decorate ceramic products and sell them to many different types of customers: boutique stores, B&Bs, hotel chains, souvenir shops, restaurants, gift shops, nurseries, online, household goods stores, baby stores – the list just goes on and on. You could even product partner with another business, i.e. sell your product packaged with the product of another business. Customers recognise that a unique handcrafted product will always be relatively more expensive than a mass-produced item so this business also offers you the potential to charge a premium selling price.

If you have no experience in ceramics but are interested in the idea, undertake a short course to understand what is involved and see if it's for you. Some institutions allow students to use their raw materials and facilities for a small fee. This is an added bonus if you want to avoid the purchase of a kiln. Alternatively you may wish to research other methods of painting and baking onto a ceramic base.

You can decorate almost anything and on-sell it to various boutique stores, retail outlets, chemists and gift shops – both online and physical stores. You could also design tourist souvenirs using ceramics and sell these to various tourist outlets all over the world. When I was holidaying in the South Island of New Zealand, I purchased a plate that had a beautiful painting of the hills and snowy mountaintops of the South Island. When I flipped it over I discovered it had been made in Australia.

You may even wish to investigate the opportunities for distributing your product range through large department stores or major giftware stores.

Ensure your product is appropriately branded with your business and contact details. People who see your product range may not necessarily be in a store. Admirers who see your product in a friend's home will want to find out who made it and possibly ask where it was purchased.

I recently came across a novel way to start a business using ceramics. Struggling to work out what I could give the grandparents for Christmas I came across a ceramic café, where adults and children could select base ceramic products and, using the store's paints and equipment, decorate them. Needless to say the grandparents received two wonderfully decorated mugs – a true keepsake.

129. Professional reunion planner

Every year groups of people decide to get together and have a reunion. All kinds of people, from high school graduates of a certain year to sailors who crewed on the same ship, will attend some type of reunion occasionally.

But organising such an event is time-consuming and daunting for amateurs, especially if one person is left to organise everything. As a result, there is now a lucrative market for professional reunion planners who will handle all the details...for a price.

To promote this business, you need to go to the source of potential reunions. Start with well-established schools that might be approached by past students enquiring about the school's assistance in organising a reunion. Once your business is established you can expand into other markets.

130. Garage organiser

Everybody wants a clean, organised garage – it's one of those weekend tasks we swear we'll get around to, but never do. Women especially nag their partners to clean up but their pleas generally go unheard. Now what if there was a service that offered to clean and organise your garage for a reasonable fee? Wouldn't you be tempted? Little start-up capital is required for a business like this other than a small amount for marketing. To get started, offer to clean out and organise your friends' garages, then take before and after pictures so you have something to show potential clients.

Once you have a well-designed brochure promoting your services, start to approach home owners. Letter drops would work well and, as you successfully complete a few jobs, word of mouth will soon spread too.

131. Online gift registry

I'll be honest: it is incredibly frustrating when you are given the wrong gift. I don't mean to sound ungrateful, but the reality is that when you are in need of something else a misguided gift can be a total waste. I am sure we have all had this experience whether we like to acknowledge it or not. So why not provide a service to help gift givers buy the right gift? A gift registry is an excellent way to ensure everyone ends up happy. You could have a wedding registry, a birth registry, a 21st, 50th and 60th registry. The receiver would sign up to the registry for a small fee and list the gifts they would like to receive. The website would need to have the capability of emailing the list to those who have been invited to the celebration. The gift giver would then go to the site and indicate the gift they intended to purchase, to prevent gifts being duplicated.

You could also sell advertising space on your site. What retailer wouldn't want to feature on a site frequented by customers intent on purchasing?

To promote your business, try putting together a press release about how it solves the problem of 'wasted gifts' and then target the media. You could also distribute your press release to wedding, parenting and women's magazines.

132. Bathtub renovator

It can be extremely expensive and time consuming to replace an outdated/worn bathtub with a brand new one. There's the cost of the new bath and fixtures, as well as the cost of the plumber to install it. If the bath is functional it's possible to refinish it; however, unless the person has experience in this area there's a real risk the bath could end up looking worse than before. This is where you come in. If you have the necessary skills, you could start a business refinishing baths. Start-up costs are low – you only need pay for the refinishing product and marketing. You can promote your services through hardware stores, plumbing supply stores and at home improvement shows. You can even refinish basins and tiles, providing a home owner with a 'brand-new' bathroom for a fraction of what it would have cost to actually buy new fittings.

Consider advertising in your local newspaper to start with. You could even offer to write an article for your local newspaper detailing the benefits of renovating your tub and how to do it properly. Be careful not to promote yourself too much as some newspapers will not print an article if it is too obviously a promotional tool. If you simply outline the finer points of renovating a bath, it's likely the reader will realise just how difficult it is and be motivated to call you in as the expert anyway.

You could also consider teaming up with your local estate agents, who could recommend your services to their clients. Transforming a worn bath into one that looks brand new could certainly help to sell a home!

Due to manpower requirements, you would be wise to confine this business to your local area, at least initially.

133. Selling advertising space

The next time you borrow a DVD check out the back of the case. There's often some blank space that's just crying out to be occupied by an advertiser. The back of a DVD case represents an excellent advertising opportunity for local businesses, particularly those situated near the DVD store. Overall the case gets looked at quite a bit so there's no reason why you couldn't sell local advertising on it. You could split the profits with each DVD store you contract with, making it a win–win proposition for them.

Local businesses will happily pay per month to appear on several thousand new releases. The best way to provide the advertising is to print the ads on removable adhesive stickers that can peel off, leaving the case ready for the next advertiser.

Think of other products this idea could work with: coffee cups distributed to cafés, napkins supplied to food courts. The possibilities are endless!

134. Google AdSense

Do you have a website that already derives traffic? Did you know you can profit from this traffic? (And I don't mean just through the sale of your products or services.) It's called AdSense and it is a program run by Google. Don't confuse this with the program

AdWords, also offered by Google. With AdWords you spend money. With AdSense you can make money.

Google AdSense is a fast and easy way for a website owner to earn money by agreeing to display relevant, unobtrusive Google ads on their website's content pages. The ads are related to what your users are looking for on your site so they do not serve as a distraction, they merely complement your content. Whenever someone clicks on the ads you host on your site, you receive a commission. You need to sign up and create an account with Google AdSense, which costs nothing but time. You will be supplied with the necessary code to place on your site and the ads will automatically populate where the code has been placed.

Keep in mind that participation in AdSense requires you to have a website. However, if you don't have one, you can still capitalise on this idea. You can just as easily create a blog by signing up for a free blog at www.blogger.com, or create and publish useful, attractive webpages using Google Page Creator, at pages.google.com. Note that if you are going to create a blog you should do your research. A popular blog with informative content will attract traffic which in turn may well click on the Google ads you host on your site.

There are several things you can do to improve your money-making potential with Google AdSense. Where you place your Google AdSense adverts makes an enormous difference to the number of clicks you get and therefore the amount you earn in commissions. For example, if you place an ad at the end of your article you can actually increase clicks. The visitor to your site is going to read the article before clicking on any adverts because the article is the reason they came to your site in the first place.

Google uses 'bots', complex algorithms, to scan web pages to locate the best adverts to serve. It is therefore important to make sure you use accurate and descriptive headings for your articles. For example, if you are writing about a technical product, use the model number in your heading. If Google does a poor job of recognising your article's topic then the adverts it displays will not be highly relevant and a visitor won't bother clicking through. Improving the relevance of the ads displayed means improving the probability that your readers will be interested in an advertisement and click on it.

Wait! What about a business plan?

By now you are probably extremely excited about the opportunities that lie before you. But before you reach for the Yellow Pages to organise your business cards, wait! Have you done a business plan?

I'll be honest, I am not a big fan of the business plan. I like to get straight into the idea at hand rather than be bogged down in research and paperwork. Nevertheless, business plans have proven to be worth their weight in gold time and time again. I have had the pleasure of meeting some very inspirational entrepreneurs who have had some amazing ideas.

But their downfall has been letting excitement and enthusiasm get in the way of proper planning. They never completed a business plan and, as a result, went head-first down the financial drain. Had they completed a business plan they would more than likely have discovered the important changes they needed to make for their business idea to succeed.

If, like me, you're not a planner at heart and quickly become distracted, why not consider this next important step as an adventure? You're off to discover the promised land! The business plan is the analysis of just how feasible your business is, so look at this next crucial step as if you are doing market research – because that's all it really is. Essentially the following topics should be covered and discussed in your business plan:

_ target market
_ your competitors
_ product assessment
_ marketing
_ production
_ financial analysis.

What follows is a brief snapshot of what you need to consider. I have not gone into great detail because it would make this book simply far too long. I suggest you go to your library and take out a few good titles that focus solely on creating a business plan. For now here is an overview of the important areas you will need to look at in order to assess the feasibility of your idea and generate a credible business plan.

1. Target market

Identifying your target market is the very first step in assessing the feasibility of your idea. If you don't have a viable target market, you certainly won't have a viable idea. Assessing the potential target market requires greater analysis than simply confirming a group of consumers exist that would probably purchase your product. There are many other considerations you need to take on board that can affect the feasibility of your idea. You need to have, as a bare minimum, an understanding of what would motivate a consumer to purchase your product.

Assess the target market at the idea stage

_ Evaluating your potential target market will help you to assess your ability to sell your product or service. If you cannot identify a group of people whose needs your product or service will successfully satisfy then it's more than likely you should either consider pursuing another idea or identify how you need to modify your product or service so that it does successfully satisfy the needs of a target market.

_ Assessing your target market could lead to valuable enhancements and modifications to your business concept. If you adopt the principle 'the customer is always right', then you will certainly gain a greater understanding of the ability of your product or service to satisfy their needs.

_ Through a thorough understanding of who represents your target market you will be able to articulate your marketing strategy better. The successful delivery of the right marketing message is solely determined by your understanding of who your target market is, what they do, where they do it, how they do it, and so on. By understanding your target market you will be able to create tailored marketing strategies to attract those customers who are more likely to purchase your product. This will ensure valuable resources are used effectively.

_ Identifying and understanding the needs of your potential target market will provide you with an opportunity to identify where you can exploit the weaknesses of your competitors.

_ Understanding who your target market is will provide vital customer intelligence that can be used to find better ways to satisfy the needs of the target market.

You can see from this by no means exhaustive list that there is substantial justification for identifying the potential consumers that constitute your target market and getting to know and understand their needs thoroughly.

A common mistake budding entrepreneurs make is to categorise their target market as anyone who will purchase their product, hoping to maximise sales. Looking at the bigger picture, this categorisation is fundamentally flawed. You must be specific about to whom you intend to sell your product. If you aim to sell to just anyone chances are some people will purchase your product and their needs won't be fully satisfied. In turn they'll be less likely to recommend your product; in fact, they may even caution their friends, family and associates against purchasing your product or service. Negative feedback is the quickest way to stifle potential sales. In the long term it is better to target customers who will wholeheartedly benefit from your product or service, since it is these customers who will become your own indirect sales team. Your overall marketing strategy should be based on the benefits gained from using your product. The best marketing approaches are those based on the single most important benefit statement.

Identifying your target market

To identify your target market you need to look at the features and benefits of your product. A feature is a characteristic or attribute that comes with the purchase of the product. For example, if a car comes with air-conditioning it is a feature, whereas the benefit is that it helps the consumer to stay cool and regulate their body temperature.

Features are valuable as they enhance the product. However, benefits are what motivate consumers to buy. It is important to be able to describe fully the features of your product so your customers understand precisely what you're offering. Features of a toothbrush, for example, might include a tongue cleaner, flexible head, contoured bristles, etc.

Benefits are based on the result of having used the product. For each feature of your product, ask yourself, 'What does the customer really get from the feature?' The benefit of a flexible head is the ability to brush hard-to-reach areas in the mouth, removing plaque that causes bacteria. The best marketing approach for a toothbrush with a flexible head, contoured bristles and a tongue cleaner would be based around the idea of preventing periodontal disease.

By understanding the benefits your product has to offer you can begin to understand which consumers will be motivated to buy it. Completing a table similar to the one below will help you to identify your possible target market. In one column, list the features of your product. In the next column, list the benefits each feature yields to the buyer. A few examples are provided:

Product	Feature	Benefit	Possible target market
Orange juice	Added vitamins, iron and calcium	Healthier altern-ative; helps provide consumers extra immunity; builds body's defences	Health-conscious
Mobile phone	Larger buttons	Easier to use	The elderly who may suffer from arthritis and/or sight problems
Moisturiser	SPF 30+	Added ingredient skin protection from harmful sun rays; reduces ageing effects of the sun	Consumers aged 30+ who are concerned about reducing the effects/signs of ageing
Car	Reverse camera	Increases driver safety by enhancing visibility behind the car, making it safer for occupants and pedestrians alike Invaluable aid to assist with the tricky task of hooking up a trailer	Parents, fisher-men, campers, motorbike enthusiasts – those who have a need for a trailer

2. Your competitors

Once you've decided a worthwhile target market exists you should now turn your attention to your competition. You need to consider the feasibility of your idea in terms of the industry you'll be operating within, including the direct and indirect competition. The research you undertake on the industry and your competitors will help form your competitive strategy.

Few businesses operate in a vacuum; within every industry

there will be various competitors, trends, threats and opportunities you'll need to contend with. You could find, after a small amount of research and investigation, that your business concept isn't viable due to a number of unattractive factors characterising the proposed industry, e.g. fierce competition and future changes that will affect the strength of the industry.

When I established my wedding photography business I never once considered the future of the wedding industry, let alone the competition. I made a common mistake – believing I was going to succeed by simply doing a better job than my competitors. In my mind I was going to provide the best wedding photography service, the best-designed contemporary wedding albums and so on. Overall, I was simply going to surpass my competition because I was going to do it better. Once word spreads, clients would flock to me. How naïve was I?

In reality there are thousands of photographers – 'wannabe' photographers, amateurs and professionals – dabbling in the wedding photography industry, offering the same product and service. The only variable is the level of quality. The competition was fierce. There were just too many photographers to compete with, all trying to secure clients (which was a feat in itself).

I also failed to recognise emerging new technology and trends in the photography industry, such as digital cameras and mini in-house theatres. These changes had a dramatic impact on the success of my business. Perhaps if I'd done a little research into the future of the industry I would have foreseen the pending technological change and probably would have purchased the equipment that has since revolutionised the industry.

I initially struggled to find clients and establish word-of-mouth referrals. There were just too many photographers for the customer to choose from. I learnt an important lesson from this mistake: review your industry and the level of competitiveness before jumping in boots and all. I failed to notice that the industry I was about to enter was extraordinarily competitive, which meant I had a lot of hard work ahead of me to establish and differentiate my business.

You, however, have the opportunity to climb a much easier mountain by assessing your competition and the industry you will operate in before you make any further commitment to your business idea.

Realistically assess your intended industry and the competition

_ It would be pointless to enter an industry and find that your resources are wasted on battling with large competitors to gain the smallest proportion of market share.

_ There may be significant problems within the industry that could affect the success of your product. For example, the need to adhere to a high level of government regulation (red tape) can be costly.

_ Has the industry already boomed? It's difficult to build a profitable and sustainable business in an industry that has already peaked.

_ Researching the industry will highlight any significant risks and issues associated with it. This will give you the opportunity to plan and devise strategies proactively to overcome any potential difficulties.

_ It's important to know and understand exactly who you'll be competing with, as this will help you to determine if you can effectively compete.

_ You need to ascertain the scope of the opportunity at hand. There's little point in establishing a business if there's little or no opportunity within the industry to compensate for the effort and cost of setting up operations.

_ A thorough understanding of your competitors and the industry will help you to identify areas where you could improve on your business idea.

_ By reviewing the products offered by competitors, you can make judgements and comparisons that could lead to value-added changes to your business concept.

_ Your assessment could reveal any geographical areas where there's an unsatisfied need that has been neglected or overlooked by competitors. It's quite possible that one of your main competitors has overlooked a certain area of the market, purely because the cost to service such a market outweighs the financial reward. However, this may not be the case for your business, and the untapped need may be your niche or entry into the industry.

What are direct and indirect competitors?

Imagine for a moment you've turned your idea into a reality; now consider who the competitors are that you're directly and indirectly competing with. Who else is offering what you offer? Identify the top five direct and indirect competitors currently operating within the industry as these are the main competitors who could potentially impact on the feasibility of your idea.

Direct competitors are those companies and individuals who sell the same or similar products. For example, Coca-Cola directly competes with Pepsi.

Indirect competitors sell the products that can be a substitute for yours. For example, Coca-Cola indirectly competes with other beverages such as water, juice, milk, tea, coffee and so on.

Consider their strengths (what they do well) and their weaknesses (what they don't do so well). This will help you to identify areas of potential opportunity as well as the scope of the available opportunity. There may be areas of the market where neither the direct nor indirect competitors have actually successfully satisfied the needs of the target market. This niche in the market represents an excellent opportunity for you to enter and operate successfully within an industry.

Who are your direct and indirect competitors?

There are a number of ways to gain information to help you identify who your direct and indirect competitors are. In some cases it may be as simple as a walk to the local shopping centre, a visit to a few of the local markets or just simply booting up your computer and surfing your way around the Internet. Here are some ways in which you can research your direct and indirect competitors.

_ Library search – visit your local library as they may have industry journals and trade publications featuring your possible competitors. Ask the librarians for assistance in tracking down information on possible competitors.

_ Networking – join industry associations or business groups. While you may still be in the evaluation stage of your idea, consider joining those networking groups affiliated with your industry and competitors. This is also a great way to not only source information on your competition, but to also keep abreast of changes in the industry and market developments.

_ Internet – the web offers a rich source of information. Use Internet search engines such as Google to find information that will lead you to your competitors' websites. These websites are often very revealing – full of competitive intelligence that can be used to refine and articulate your competitive strategy.

_ Industry and/or trade journals – industry-specific periodicals are a useful source of information and competitor advertisements.

_ White and Yellow Pages – your library or local post office should stock the White Pages and Yellow Pages directories for all cities and regions. You can also do your research online.

_ Statistics and market research – look for sites that sell market research and current statistics; for example, in the UK you could frequent the Department of Statistics, www.statistics.gov.uk Worldwide, you might consider World Ometers, www.worldometers.info It is also a good idea to check online newspapers, as quite often the articles will contain statistics quoted in various reports. This is an ideal source for leads you can use to obtain further information. Many online newspapers have a search function you can use to search on relevant terms.

_ Speak to the customers and/or the suppliers of the competition – see if you can talk to your competitors' customers. Get a feel for what the customers think of the business. Are they happy with the supplier of the product? If not, what could be improved? If the customers are happy, ask why they are satisfied with the supplier. This is particularly easy if you're selling to a retailer who is then selling the product to the customer. It's best to phone or visit a retailer when you want to obtain such information on your competitors.

When evaluating your own idea it's important to evaluate what the competitors are actually doing.

Make the investment and purchase the competitors' products. Analyse what they do and how.

Take the products apart, carefully look at how they're made, packaged, the shape, the quality, the materials, the products' durability, the value provided, what's special and not so special about them.

If it's a service, take note of what's done and how well it's done, the environment the service is provided in.

If any products are used in the delivery of the service consider those products as well. At the completion of your analysis consider how you would rate your experience of each competitor's product or service.

This is vital competitor intelligence that can be used to further redefine and shape your idea.

A great idea is to 'mystery shop' your competition or arrange for a friend or colleague to visit a competitor and report on the experience. These visits can be a rich source of information on how busy the business seems; the quality of the layout, décor and signage; the friendliness of the staff; and the range of products and services.

When I realised I had to restructure the direction of my wedding photography business, I decided to do some undercover research on my competition. My husband and I posed as an engaged couple and visited at least ten photographers, my direct competitors. We watched what they did, how they did it, what they offered in the way of refreshments, brochures and so forth. We were researching not only the product but the entire experience my competitors were offering their clients. I was able to see and assess first-hand the level of competition I had to contend with and, more importantly, what I would have to do to turn my business around and appeal to the same target market.

3. Product assessment

It saddens me to see the number of people starting businesses selling the same old product already available on the market; these businesses are generally known as copycats. If you want to be successful in business your product must have a strong 'unique selling proposition' (USP), also referred to as a 'competitive advantage'. This section will help you to define your USP and assess if it's feasible to market a product given the circumstances that define your USP.

In order to change the course of my wedding photography business so that it would grow, I needed to revise my own product and service offering. This was an expensive exercise since I had already spent thousands of pounds on product samples – 30-page 'display' promotional wedding albums in a magazine layout. I later realised this exercise was a waste of money. My target market didn't care about the expensive albums; instead they were looking for a photographer they could have a personal connection with and who could take great shots on the day. As a majority of the members of my target market preferred to create their own wedding albums, they only needed me to supply the photographs. Had I correctly identified who my target market was and who I was really competing with from the very beginning, I would have recognised the products and services my target market really needed. I definitely wouldn't have spent so much money creating display albums to try to sell a product my target market clearly didn't want.

Assessing the feasibility of your product follows on from your understanding of your target market and the competitive environment. By this point you should be well aware of the needs your product or service will satisfy through the benefits it provides and you should have a thorough understanding of who represents your target market. You should also have a solid understanding of what your competition has to offer and what you'll need to do to compete successfully within your industry. Now is the time to define and assess the feasibility of your product or service in terms of its potential to generate sales successfully and deliver a profit. What is your unique selling proposition? What is the core benefit of your product or service? And finally, what is the actual and augmented product or service? It's important to co-ordinate each level of your product or service so that you can provide the greatest perceived value for money.

Business owners unfortunately often assume the customer is solely concerned with the core benefit provided by the product or service. They focus exclusively on designing and building the consumable elements of their product. For example, a manufacturer of a vacuum cleaner may focus on creating a vacuum cleaner that cleans more effectively, when in reality this may not be the only benefit sought by the target market. While decisions related to the consumable parts of the product are extremely important, the totality of the vacuum cleaner consists of more than what's consumed. Your total product offering should be broken down into three key parts:

a. core benefit
b. actual product or service
c. augmented product or service.

a. Core benefit

The core benefit is the purpose for which a consumer buys the product or service. It should satisfy the target market's highest perceived need. Generally speaking, the core benefit is intangible. At the very heart of your product or service is determining the key or core benefits your product or service will provide in relation to the unsatisfied needs of your target market. For example, if I purchased soup from my local supermarket, the soup inside the container provides the core benefit of a full stomach – it alleviates my hunger. If I go to a beautician for a set of acrylic nails, I expect to feel beautiful or at least well groomed when I walk out. Once you understand and appreciate your product or service's core benefit, the rest of the offering can be developed.

Product	Core benefit purchased
A builder's drill	A hole
Beauty products such as lipstick	Hope, confidence, beauty
Camera	Memories
Vacuum cleaner	Cleanliness

b. Actual product or service

The actual product or service is what the consumer holds in their hand or the result of the service. In the previous examples, the container the soup comes in is the actual product and the application of the acrylic nails is the service provided. While the consumable product or service is, in most cases, the most critical of all decisions, the actual product or service includes many separate decisions such as features, branding, packaging, labelling and more, which can all serve to influence a consumer's purchasing decision. It's important to understand that, even though the core benefit of your product or service satisfies the highest needs of your target market, the actual product or service plays an important role in satisfying the lesser needs, which may well become the deciding factors between competing products or services.

Following on from our example of the vacuum cleaner, how

176

the vacuum cleaner is designed, the features it includes – ease of use, how it grips the floor, how the head swivels, the level of suction, the size of the actual unit, whether it's bagless or not, whether it's manufactured by a well-known brand or a relative unknown – are all important aspects to consider. In terms of the beautician, the type of acrylic nails the beautician uses, how she applies these, how long they are expected to last, and whether she uses hypoallergenic acrylic are all important features of the service provided. The successful co-ordination of the attributes of the actual product or service in line with the needs of your target market could see your product or service become the consumer's preferred choice.

c. Augmented product or service

The augmented product or service takes the marketing of your product or service one step further as it's the non-physical part of the product or service. It usually consists of lots of added value, for which you can charge the consumer a premium. The augmented product or service involves surrounding the actual product or service with goods and services that provide additional value to the consumer's purchase. Again these factors alone may not be the key reason that leads the consumer to purchase; however, the inclusion of these items can most definitely influence the consumer's decision. Items considered part of the augmented product or service include: guarantee, warranty, customer service, complementary products, accessibility and so on. In the case of the beautician, she may guarantee that if a nail chips within three weeks she will provide free repair, or she may offer free touch-ups between appointments.

It's absolutely vital to take the time to assess your product or service range in terms of its totality. What you decide to add to or omit from your total product or service offering impacts both on your ability to appeal to your target market and satisfy their needs and on your ability to generate a profit successfully. You'll need to balance the needs of your target market, your competitor's offerings and your ability to derive a profit with the co-ordination of product or service attributes.

What are the product attributes that are important to your potential target market? You'll only know the answer to this question if you've thoroughly researched the needs of your target market.

The information provided in the previous sections should highlight exactly what would influence the purchasing decisions of your target customer and what wouldn't.

If the answer isn't yet clear, go back to your target customer and start delving a little deeper into their needs.

If you're considering producing children's clothing, ask about fabrics, stitches, appliqué and packaging.

If you're producing a food-based product, find out what tastes and textures are important, the types of ingredients preferred (organic or not), etc. If you're going to deliver a product, find out how the customer expects delivery.

For a cleaning product would the customer prefer to use one that was environmentally friendly?

It's the additional attention to detail that will see your product or service win the hearts of your target market.

4. Marketing

How will you successfully market your product in a way that will best generate sales? Developing and implementing a successful marketing strategy is essential for the survival of any business. The identification of your target market, the benefits provided by your product or service and your competitive strategy all play a major role in defining and shaping your marketing strategy, which is why you should complete those areas of your business plan first.

Many businesses fail because they don't strategically market their business. If you cannot market your product or service properly you'll struggle to make sales and succeed. It's also far smarter to consider your marketing strategy now rather than to invest in starting up a business only to find you're struggling to appeal to the right target customer or, worse, cannot afford to market it successfully. Marketing is all about being creative, coming up with innovative and resourceful ways to promote your business and distribute your product or service at a price willingly accepted by your target consumer.

One of the more challenging roles you'll undertake when evaluating the potential of your idea is to developing a marketing strategy that will successfully launch your product or service into the market. Firstly, it's important to understand how your target market treats the purchase decisions they face. Some purchases are straightforward and are made every day. For example, buying food usually requires little thought. Other decisions are far more complex and require a greater level of consideration and analysis – such as the purchase of a house. I have yet to meet someone who has purchased the first home they saw based on one inspection. Your potential marketing strategy will vary depending on the degree of decision-making required for different buying situations. You also need to take into account the role emotion will play in a consumer's decision-making process. For example, some people might be motivated to buy a certain food product out of fear that other products might not be as healthy or good for their child.

Your marketing research should cover the following topics:

a. pricing
b. distribution channels
c. promotion.

a. Pricing

You'll need to decide on an appropriate selling price. This decision is a delicate balancing act. It's critical that your selling price is set in line with the target market's perception of value, otherwise you may well create the wrong impression. At the same time you will need to identify a price that takes into account the expenses incurred in the operation of the business and still ensures you derive a reasonable profit margin.

Pricing is a topic you need to take time to understand and

appreciate. A selling price is basically the result of the relationship between value, perception and need. Customers base their purchasing decisions on perceived value and their level of need. Your optimal selling price is directly proportional to what your target market is prepared to pay for your product. How much do they value the totality of your product? How well does it satisfy their needs? Again you can see why it's so important to understand fully your target market so that you understand what they perceive as genuine value. It's all very well setting a selling price you'd like your product to return, but if your target market is not prepared to pay then you'll have a problem.

It is a very good idea to research what selling price you can actually charge as this can have many implications for the overall feasibility of your idea. When I first started my photography business, I assumed that, like the well-established and popular wedding photographers, I would also have customers prepared to pay upwards of £3,000 for a personally designed wedding album. I could not have been more wrong! If only I had actually done a little market research, I would have realised the £3,000 price tag is generally commanded by those who have had extensive experience in the industry and who have built a solid brand. I suspect that if I had discovered what my target market was really prepared to pay for my services in the analysis stage of the idea, I probably would not have started the business in the first place.

More often than not potential business owners fail to consider their selling price and how this will affect the viability of their product or service. If you take the time to research what price range is generally accepted by the target market, you won't run the risk of out-pricing yourself, or under-pricing and finding you're making a loss instead of a profit.

The characteristics, features and benefits – the totality of your product as discussed previously – will also affect the selling price you can set. If you intend to offer a product of lesser quality, one that is widely available and is cheap to produce, then you should consider setting a lower level selling price in line with the consumer's perceived level of value. For example, many of those Poundland, Bargain Basement shops set lower prices for their stock because their products are relatively cheap to produce. They're produced en masse, they provide a core benefit and in some cases the actual product and augmented product are not major features. These types of shops are not targeting those who are prepared to pay for brand-name products. Instead they are targeting customers with less disposable income who are prepared to compromise on the quality, features and style of a product, provided it's still functional. If the bargain shops decided to enter the market appealing to the high-end consumer, they would soon find their businesses in trouble.

Additional factors that will impact on your pricing decision include:

_ What's the selling price set by competitors?
_ What prices do you set for wholesale customers as opposed to retail customers?
_ Do you provide volume discounts? If so, what can you offer?
_ Do you offer seasonal pricing? For example, it is cheaper to stay in a hotel during off-peak seasons.

The table below will help you to differentiate which characteristics determine whether a product or service attracts a higher or lower selling price.

Lower selling price	Higher selling price
Widely available	Handmade – unique, one-off
Mass produced	Well-known brand name
Lesser quality	Rare/scarce raw materials used in production
Lower level of functionality	
Little packaging and/or branding, if any	Product is well packaged – 'appearance'
High level of quality – made to last	Extra features, functionality and benefits compared to competitors' products
	Sold in boutique outlets not large chain/department stores

b. Distribution channels

You'll need to decide where you're going to sell the product or service, your distribution channel. This is an important decision as it can impact on the potential of your idea to generate sales and derive a profit. There are many ways and means to distribute a product or service – refer to the list below – but the optimal distribution channel is the one that is most in line with the needs of your customers.

Some examples of distribution channels are:

_ direct to customer – local markets, shopping centre carts, party plan
_ shopping channels on pay TV
_ direct marketing company
_ website and/or eBay
_ sales agent/broker
_ distribution agent
_ wholesaler
_ retailers – large department stores, boutique stores
_ exporting.

When evaluating the feasibility of your idea you need to balance the needs of your target market with the impact each distribution channel will have on your potential profit margin. The following are some examples of the decisions you may need to make:

_ Where are members of your target market located geographically? Which distribution channel will provide the most cost-effective access to your target market?
_ Where does your target market wish to purchase your product or service?
_ Can you convince your target market to purchase through a more cost effective distribution channel, i.e. if they purchase through a retail store could you convince them to purchase through the Internet? If so, what would this strategy cost?
_ What are the costs of using various distribution channels? For example, selling through your own website has far less impact on your profit margin than selling through a retailer who will take a 25 to 50 per cent cut of the sale.
_ Which distribution channel offers the greatest level of market awareness, enabling your product or service to also gain market penetration?
_ What are the dominant channels of distribution used by your competitors? Can you also tap into these channels? And if so, what impact could this have on your profit margin? For example, large corporate businesses will enjoy better returns using large department stores for distribution, because they can compete en masse; whereas a smaller business, which lacks economies of scale,

could find the commissions paid through this distribution channel would greatly reduce their profit potential.

> It's also important to note that you don't have to stick to the same distribution channel you start out with.
> The initial means of distributing your product may very well change as more people learn about the benefits of your product and your business begins to grow.
> Don't be concerned that where you begin to distribute your product or service is where your business will end.
> Your initial distribution channel is a starting point – like a toddler beginning to learn to walk, you need to take baby steps.
> Let's look again at the case of Sue Ismiel, the mother of three who created Nad's Hair Removal Gel in 1992. Sue started out selling her product at Sydney's Flemington Market. Since then Sue has managed to develop Nad's into a leading international distributor of personal care products, which are also sold in Australian chemists and grocery stores.

c. Promotion

Your promotional strategy defines how you'll encourage market awareness of your product or service. It should set out how you intend to position your product or service and the message you'll communicate to your target market. By what means will the message be delivered? TV commercial, radio, newspaper, word-of-mouth? The way in which you promote your business could affect the feasibility of your idea, but the right promotional strategy is entirely dependent on the idea at hand.

One of the biggest obstacles and challenges facing a new

business is to get customers to try your product or service. What do you have to do to convince your target market to buy, buy, buy? Unfortunately, in most cases, a mere advertisement is not enough to seduce the target market to act. You need to promote your business consistently. How you promote your product or service can be likened to a recipe: each promotional tool is an ingredient that, if varied, can modify the outcome. Promotional activities generally have a financial cost so you need to be certain that you can afford to promote your product in a manner that will speak directly to your target market. Obviously if you cannot afford a promotional campaign that will effectively reach your target market then I'd suggest you reconsider the idea.

Some promotional decisions you may need to consider include:

_ What are the most favourable benefits of your product you should consider promoting (your message)?

_ Which promotional channels will provide the greatest level of awareness, connecting you to your target market?

_ What resources do you have to carry out the promotional strategy?

_ How will you successfully communicate your message – advertising and/or word of mouth?

_ What's the core selling proposition and how can it be communicated most effectively to customers – advertising, PR, direct sales?

_ Is the promotional budget adequate to achieve objectives?

Below is a list of various promotional tools you could consider using.

Remember that each one will incur a different cost.

_ Public Relations agent
_ direct mail services
_ marketing agency
_ brochures/catalogues/promotional stationery
_ promotional gifts
_ signage
_ bus stops
_ billboards
_ shopping centres

_ merchandising displays
_ samples: – samples to potential retailers
_ show bags, i.e. Bounty Bags
_ advertising:
_ magazine
_ newspaper
_ television
_ online – banner ads/newsletters
_ Yellow Pages
_ radio
_ trade shows/exhibitions
_ website – online e-marketing, i.e. newsletter and database
_ website – domain registration and hosting
_ website design and development
_ networking – cost to join associations and attend functions
_ product partnering
_ packaged offer
_ voucher and coupons.

When assessing your potential promotional strategy it's worth remembering that the one who does the buying is not necessarily the user of what's bought. Others may be involved in the buying decision in addition to the end user of the product and this can impact on the creation of a potential promotional strategy. For example, in the past many family car manufacturers predominantly promoted their cars to men. Of late, however, there's been a change to whom the car manufacturers promote their product range. It would appear the manufacturers have realised that at the forefront of any significant major family purchase is the woman. Consequently, family car promotional campaigns are tailored for and targeted at women. Ford's television commercial for the Ford Territory featuring mums in their 'rigs' at a school drop-off is a great example of this.

5. Production

The next step is to consider your production strategy. It's important to assess your ability to manufacture the product and the alternatives that exist if you need outside help. The financial repercussions from failing to consider how to best produce a product can be severe.

Often I find budding entrepreneurs have a great idea, go through the expense of registering a business name, a domain name, and designing their business card and stationery only to find they cannot actually purchase the stock they need for their business. In one instance, associates found that because they intended to resell the stock online, a number of suppliers refused to supply on the grounds they believed this distribution channel would dilute their brand position in the marketplace. Even though we live in a commercial world don't simply assume you'll have access to anything and everything.

Early research will help you to identify potential problems and solutions. You may even find that you discover an alternative, cost effective way to produce your product. In the initial stages of my photography business, I decided to use only professional film and only professional labs to develop my film and reproduce my reprints. I wanted to follow in the footsteps of the professionals I was trying to emulate. Then one day I urgently required a reprint and the professional lab was too busy for my deadline. In desperation I used a regular photo lab in a major department store. The lab was able to produce my photographs at a superior quality to that of the professional lab and for a quarter of the price. With this discovery I decided to do a little experiment using everyday, run-of-the-mill film at a fraction of the cost of a roll of professional film, and again, the quality was still just as impressive. I more than halved my production costs and there was no detectable change in quality in the eyes of my target market.

There are three ways to produce your product:

1. fully or partially outsource the manufacturing of the product
2. produce the product yourself
3. sell or license the design/idea to a larger manufacturer.

Of course, this section of your business plan is less relevant if you are offering a service. However, in this instance it's a good idea to consider the alternative choices available that will help you to deliver the service in an affordable and satisfactory manner that satisfies your target market's needs. For example, as a bookkeeper I deliver a service: balanced books with timely, accurate information. However, when establishing this business, I had to decide how I would deliver this service. The well-known accounting applications available each had different functions that could either increase or decrease my ability to deliver the service in a cost-effective manner. It was up to me to determine which software was the best fit for my business.

Production considerations

_ Potential production issues may be uncovered when you research how you'll produce your product. It's wise to have addressed any possible problems before you actually enter into full-scale production. Production problems can include:

_ minimum order restrictions
_ difficulty locating suppliers
_ quality control.
_ Having a full appreciation of how you'll produce your product will help you identify the level of cash flow required to sustain your business in its early stages.
_ Understanding how you'll produce your product will help you to accurately calculate necessary product costings, budgeted gross margins and other important financial calculations.
_ You may need to consult with a professional industrial designer to help you produce your product. A good industrial designer will have experience on their side and will be able to make valuable suggestions to aid and enhance the design of your product. They may also provide leads for possible manufacturers and suppliers.

Speaking to various suppliers will help you to explore opportunities to further improve your idea. Some suppliers are only too happy to give valuable advice and direction based on their many years of experience.

The councils within your region will have different by-laws that govern the town planning requirements for the operation of a home-based business. It's important that you contact your local council, specifically the town planning department, to obtain an official set of guidelines. It's important you clearly understand how they may affect your business. You might think this is unnecessary but remember that the council has the power to veto your business if you don't seek the proper approval, licences or permits to operate your business from home. All it would take for them to find out about your home business is for a disgruntled neighbour to make a call and complain, even if was only over something small such as signage on your fence. In the long run it's much less expensive to play it safe. So visit your local council and discuss your plans for your business. Finally, make sure you obtain any agreements or advice from the council in writing.

6. Financial analysis

Before you can calculate the potential profitability of your idea, you need to have considered all facets of the idea. Then, and only then, will you be in a position to consider its financial feasibility. The financial analysis of your business idea will determine:

_ how long it will take to make a profit and how many units you'll need to sell or services you'll need to carry out to break even

_ how much reserve cash you'll need to keep the business afloat during start-up phase
_ what level of investment is required just to start the business
_ what profit margins you could expect to earn and whether this is commensurate with the effort required.

To work out the overall profitability of your business, you need to take the sum of your total expenses away from the forecast sales revenue. Depending on the complexity of your idea, you may well need to cost out various marketing and production strategies to realise the optimal strategy and evaluate your idea based on these results. It's important to cost all possible scenarios so you can make an informed and accurate decision on the optimal strategy to pursue. With my first print run for my book *Show Mummy the Money* I had a choice as to how I could distribute the book – bookstores, online, or both. I had to cost out both scenarios to conclude which would provide me with the greatest opportunity for success.

At this stage you can only plan for what you know and believe could happen. Calculating an estimated profit is merely another means to help you assess the idea at hand.

To help you consider the financial viability of your idea, in the table on the following page I have included all the possible expenses you could incur and which should form part of your financial analysis.

Business Start-up
Business registration
Accounting fees
Any necessary business licences and/or permits related to your product
Insurance
Training and education
Bank account fees, credit card facility
Payment processing equipment, credit card machine and stationery
Any membership, subscriptions or association fees

Stationery Expenses
Design of logo
Letterhead
Envelopes
Invoices
Postage
With Compliments slips
Business cards

Office Set-up Expenses
Computer hardware, i.e. PC
Software: accounting package such as Quicken Books or MYOB
Computer equipment, e.g. scanner
Furniture: desk/chair
Office supplies: paper, pens, pencils, calculator
Filing system, i.e. folders and dividers
Drawers
Phone: answering machine or voice messaging service

Expenses
Advertising/Promotional Expenses
Advertising expenses
Direct marketing expenses, brochures/flyers
Exhibition fees
Catalogues
Cost to list website in various search engines
Signage
Actual market research
Visual merchandise, display costs, racks, cases

Website – Set-up expenses
Domain name registration for website
Internet access
Website annual hosting fees
Website design

Product-related Costs
Product samples
Cost to lease a shopping mall cart
Packaging costs
Price tags
Cost of stock
Freight for importing stock
Customs and importation charges on imported stock
Freight costs to move stock nationally
Storage costs for stock

Before I conclude this chapter, here's a word of advice. Whatever you do, always test, test, test and measure. After you have researched your idea and are ready to launch your business, consider the scale of your launch. Do you have the correct systems in place to test and measure your success? Investing your life savings into a business concept without testing it first is asking for trouble. You could very well save a small fortune by launching your business on a smaller scale, giving you the opportunity to correct any possible errors before you have established a reputation or sunk all your funds. A perfect example of this comes to mind.

Two years after I launched *Show Mummy the Money*, I decided to expand the book into a magazine. I broadened the content to include not only how to make money, but also how to save and protect money as well. I launched a physical hard copy on a national basis, when I could have launched the magazine online – a virtual magazine. I sank a fair amount of capital into the magazine only to find it's very difficult to secure advertising revenue – the lifeblood of any magazine. Before I got to the third edition I had hit a wall, my capital had dried up and I could not secure enough advertisers to continue. While I had a great idea – as evidenced by the continual requests for copies of the magazine, even months after its demise – what I didn't test and measure was how difficult it would be to lure advertisers into a brand-new magazine. Had I launched online I would have experienced the same difficulty only I would have saved the production costs associated with physically printing the magazine.

Build systems into your business concept to ensure you are continually testing and measuring your success. The only way to satisfy the needs of a target market is to ensure you are continually improving your product or service in line with the feedback.

Getting yourself on the web

Luckily for the budding entrepreneur it has become a lot cheaper to have an online store. Only five years ago it cost more than £5,000 for a basic e-commerce site. For most small businesses a website is a must; it is an excellent marketing tool to direct customers to find out more about your products and services. More importantly though it has become one of the most cost-effective ways to gain access to a worldwide market of potential customers.

Before you go to the expense of designing and developing a website, make sure you do your research! It's absolutely vital that the website appears and functions professionally. I simply cannot stress this point enough! Your website is your shopfront so you won't get away with a poorly designed and functioning DIY website.

There are some tips and tricks to ensure you don't pay too much yet still come out with a fully functional website. Firstly, it's important you're familiar with the main e-commerce concepts, as this will enable you to consider what you need for your own business.

Domain name
Before you can publish a website or create your own business email

address you'll need to register a domain name. A domain name is the unique address that identifies the location of a website on the Internet, e.g. www.showmummythemoney.com.au is my domain name. Domain names should contain the name of a business, and usually end in .com. Registering a domain name gives you a licence to use the selected name for a specified period of time, subject to the terms and conditions defined by the registrar.

It's a good idea to check the availability of the domain name before you register the actual business name. For example, it would be pointless registering Show Mummy the Money as a business name if I couldn't secure the domain name as well. Potential customers may search for your business via your business name; if your website has a different name, then chances are customers will fail to find you.

I recommend registering all possible domain name extensions as this means no one else can capitalise on the goodwill of your business. So, in the UK for example, I would recommend that you register both .com and .co.uk for your business name. Generally domain name providers will offer the registration of both for only a little more than the cost of registering just one. Spend the extra and register both domains – you can ask your website developer to point one of the domain names to the original website, like a mirror, so that when a user types in either .co.uk or .com they arrive at the same website. If you don't register both domain name extensions, there's nothing to prevent someone anywhere in the world from registering the remaining extension and setting up shop to cash in on your reputation. Remember that when a potential online shopper searches for your business in a search engine, they will probably type in your business name. The search results will return all businesses of that name, including any who registered the domain extensions you might have neglected to purchase.

To check if the domain name you require isn't already taken, you can visit the domain name registry for your country. For example, in the UK this would be www.nic.uk and in Europe, www.eurid.eu. You can register and pay for a domain name by visiting the website of an accredited registrar or reseller. There are plenty of registrars. Note you can often get a better deal if you agree to sign up for a domain name and hosting, and some hosting providers will throw in the domain name registration for free.

To publish a website on the purchased domain name, you'll need to acquire the services of a hosting provider; many Internet domain name providers provide this service as well. A host provides you with a place to store your website. It's different from an Internet Service Provider (ISP). An ISP will allow you access to surf the net and send and receive emails, whereas a host allows you to upload your website to the Internet so the world can access it. Again there are a range of host providers, each with differing services, packages, pricing and features – you do need to take the time to read the fine print and assess the suitability of the host for your needs. For example, you'll need to ensure the hosting service caters for the potential size of your website. A website's size is measured in terms of megabytes and is affected by variables such as the level of traffic visiting the site, the number of downloads, etc. Generally speaking, if you're using the services of a professional web developer they'll organise this service for you.

Email address

A professional email address is very important. Your email address should be linked with your business. If you're serious about your business, don't use a free service such as hotmail as it simply doesn't look professional. When you register your own domain name, your ISP should be able to establish an email address using your domain name at the end. For example, my domain name is www.showmummythemoney.com.au so therefore my main email address is info@showmummythemoney.com.au. Not only will this create consistency and give a much more professional impression, but another advantage is that you can maintain the email address irrespective of which ISP you're with, thus allowing you the option to change ISPs.

Developing, designing and building a website

You have some options when it comes to the development of your website. The first is to use a professional web designer. Many website developers/designers will package up their services by offering to register your domain name, set up your email addresses, secure the services of a host provider, and finally build the website. In essence they do the lot. This option is naturally more expensive but it does take away a lot of the pain associated with DIY.

The next option is to build your website yourself (DIY). There are a number of different ways to do this. A range of different software products, such as Dreamweaver, are available for purchase, but you could also surf the net to find free software to use to build your website. Then there are pre-designed and formatted templates. These are sold by many online stores or you can also download free templates at www.freelayouts.com. However, you do need to know what you're doing when you download your template.

Another option is to use the services of a hosting provider who provides DIY software so you can generate your own site. Most hosting providers do offer this additional service for free if you are prepared to pay for their hosting services. There are some hosting providers who even supply website templates, shopping carts and many other applications to help their customers build a fully functional website, all as part of their hosting fee. This is a fantastic option if you're interested in setting up your own website on a budget; check out www.rapidhost.co.uk as an example. However, you may still need some sort of software to use the template. Check with the template provider first. Volusion, www.volusion.com, is a US-based company that offers a similar service and whose templates are already search engine optimised (SEO). SEO is one means to get your website ranked higher in a search engine request. With some of the providers like Volusion you can download a trial version of the product to see how you go. Or you could try www.register.com for as little as US $12.95 per month.

My personal preference – unless you really know what you're doing – is to get a professional designer involved, specifically someone who also specialises in e-marketing and search engine optimisation. A professional web designer will be able to set your site up correctly from the start, so you can begin capitalising on all the e-marketing opportunities offered by selling on the Internet.

Shopping carts

If you're using your website to sell products or services, you'll need to incorporate a shopping cart into your website. Bluepark, www.bluepark.co.uk, is a provider of e-commerce shopping cart software that caters for small- to medium-sized businesses looking to build or simply start an online business. One of the great things about Bluepark is you can hire the shopping cart for a month or a year; you can also organise a trial to ensure the software fits your needs. You are not locked into a two-year contract, which is great if you are only testing your concept as it substantially reduces the financial risk.

You can also choose to purchase the rights to use a shopping cart by buying the licence for the shopping cart software. However, you will need to pay for the full year irrespective of whether you decide to terminate the idea after four months of trading. Companies like Uniwin, www.uniwin.com, can sell you a licence enabling you to use their shopping cart software. There are many other shopping cart providers – Google the phrase 'shopping cart providers' and you'll see what I mean. Some even offer their services for free, like Mal's E-Commerce, www.mals-e.com

Each shopping cart provider will have software with different features and benefits so make sure your business needs are met by the selected software. Don't expect your designer to understand the needs of your customer; you should ensure for yourself that you have the right shopping cart. For example, some shopping carts will come with their own SSL certificate (see definition below), whereas with others you may have to purchase the certificate separately – these costs can soon add up.

A poor shopping cart is one of the main reasons a customer will click away from your site without making a purchase. I personally learned this lesson when I started to receive complaints from potential customers about their shopping experience on my site. When I placed an order with myself, I found their complaints were justified so I quickly changed shopping carts and now enjoy regular sales.

How a shopping cart works

The shopping cart allows the customer visiting your website to purchase. Websites with a shopping cart facility have two websites: one for the customer to place the order on (the actual website visible to the customer) and another website for the owner to access and process the orders. This second secure website is only visible to and accessible by the owner. When deciding on a shopping cart provider, be sure the facility provided is secure.

Security required for a shopping cart

It's important to ensure your website is secure, particularly if customers are providing credit card details online. In some cases you may need to purchase an SSL certificate to ensure you have a secure website for taking credit card payments. SSL stands for Secure Socket Layer, a protocol developed by Netscape for transmitting private documents via the Internet. It is a cryptographic system that uses two keys to encrypt data – a public key known to everyone and a private, or secret, key known only to the recipient of the message. The SSL certificate allows your website to display the 'padlock' that appears on secure websites in the top right-hand corner. Customers are more likely to purchase from a site with a visible padlock than one that doesn't display any sign of security. You can Google the term 'SSL certificate' and find a number of providers. Some shopping cart software providers and merchant facilitators will offer the SSL certificate as part of their package. Make sure you read the fine print and don't purchase a certificate unnecessarily.

Processing credit card payments

If you're selling products and services online you'll need to organise a means to take credit card payments. I would suggest you visit your bank and discuss what options they have available. Some banks actually provide the necessary security to your website so you won't need to purchase the SSL certificate mentioned above. One solution used by some banks is Web Advantage. This is a product that interfaces with the shopping cart on your website. Effectively, the customer makes a purchase on your website using a credit card and the credit card is automatically processed by the bank, without the business owner doing a thing. The funds from sales are automatically deposited into the bank account and the business owner is alerted as to which orders to fulfil.

If your bank is reluctant to provide merchant facilities there are alternatives such as PayPal. Simply go to www.paypal.com and click on the 'Merchant' tab. PayPal merchant facilities operate in the same manner as those facilities offered by the large banks. You'll need to obtain certification, which essentially verifies your identity, and once this has been done you'll be able to access their comprehensive manual as well as tailor the PayPal facilities to your website. It's free to register with PayPal – charges are based on the sales processed by PayPal on your behalf – and its convenience means it is a widely recognised method of payment.

The costs to use merchant facilities

It's important to consult with the merchant facility department of your bank, since all banks differ in what they offer and charge. Some factors you need to take into account include:

_ the transaction costs per sale – this is usually calculated based on a per sale basis, i.e. some banks will charge 15p to 30p for each sale deposited into your account

_ the merchant facilities rates – some banks will charge between 1.7 and 2 per cent per sale for using the bank's merchant facilities, i.e. processing the sale onto the customer's credit card

_ any minimum monthly fees for the provision of the merchant facilities

_ the establishment fees – it can cost up to £300 to establish the merchant facility; however, bear in mind that it's usually the IT department of the bank that is responsible for integrating the merchant facilities into your website, so your 'start-up fee' is paying for a worthy service

_ the cancellation fees – if you decide you no longer require the bank's merchant facilities

_ the process for charge backs – where a customer disputes the credit card transaction processed on their credit card.

E-marketing

Websites are a great tool to market your products or services cost-effectively to potential customers. However, with any e-marketing campaign, you must obtain the customer's permission first before embarking on any communication strategy. You can set your website up to easily obtain such permission, i.e. through opt-in subscription to newsletters, catalogues and so forth.

A properly executed e-marketing campaign can help any new start-up to grow as:

_ it can help promote by word of mouth since emails are easily forwarded

_ it will help your business to foster, develop and cultivate

relationships by regularly engaging the customer
_ it's a cost-effective means of communication.

Your website should provide a way for customers to submit their details. For example, you could offer your customers the opportunity to receive a monthly newsletter. You may even wish to collect the customer's details according to their interests and preferences. This will provide you with the opportunity to tailor the information you communicate to the subscriber.

A monthly newsletter can also be used to keep your current customers informed of the introduction of any new products or services you may have developed or any specials they might like to take advantage of. A monthly newsletter can provide a business with the opportunity to explain and better educate a customer on a particular topic, products, services and so on. Providing valuable and important information can also be what converts a potential customer into an actual customer.

E-marketing providers such as www.constantcontact.com can help you to design and set up a professional-looking newsletter as well as manage your subscribers.

Offer your customers a discount when they sign up as this will provide them with further motivation to make a purchase. At the same time it will help build your database of potential customers. Borders provide an excellent example of e-marketing at work. At the close of your purchase with Borders, the sales assistant will ask whether you are a member of their mailing list. When you sign up to their mailing list you receive an e-newsletter every Friday and every newsletter offers a discount. Borders' e-newsletter encourages recipients to make their purchases at their store. I personally refrain from making any book, magazine or music-related purchases until I receive my Borders e-newsletter to see if I can gain a discount on my purchases. It also drives traffic into the store where customers can consider other purchases as well. The discount is generally only valid for a certain period of time thus providing a compelling justification for the consumer to act.

A website is fantastic if it is set up right and operated effectively. It's also worth mentioning that a website can be high maintenance, particularly if you regularly have to update it and find new information to keep it interesting. If you have properly researched your target market you should be very clear about whether a website would be of assistance to your business or not.

Conclusion

I hope that by now you have found your own seed, which you can continue to develop and grow into a sustainable and profitable business. This book is designed to provide you with inspiration and insights. Unfortunately, I can't give you all the answers because everyone has different needs, personal circumstances and interests. The best I can do is to open your eyes to what you could be – your future potential.

Whichever idea you end up pursuing, be sure you are passionate about what you intend to do. As I said at the beginning, passion is the lifeblood of any successful entrepreneur. Without it you will find it difficult to get any business idea off the ground, simply because people – whether they are potential customers for your product or service, or the bank manager whom you might need to convince to give you a loan – will only buy in if they believe you are passionate about what you are doing. Few of us will buy from someone if we sense their enthusiasm is faked.

Irrespective of what you do from here, I would like to leave you with the best piece of business advice you will ever get.

Do your RESEARCH, TEST AND MEASURE before you make any substantial financial commitment.

It doesn't matter how great you think your idea is, or how great you think you are, you must research your idea properly. The level of research you do before starting your business will dictate your level of success or failure.

I have personally learned how detailed research and thorough analysis can contribute to the success of a business. When I started my wedding photography business in 2000 I made every fundamental mistake I could – I didn't do enough research. Years later, after I had successfully grown my wedding photography business, I decided to write about the research I should have done before I started my business. I found that undertaking this critical research during the operation of my business probably delayed my success by two years. Don't make the business mistakes made by so many others.

Hindsight is not a wonderful thing; it's a source of regret.

Go to your library and read up on business plans. Prepare your own business plan and, most importantly, cost out exactly what it will take financially to get your idea off the ground. Several successful business people have said to me that when preparing the numbers you should multiply the answer by three since this is generally a more realistic figure to go with. It will always cost more than you expect. It will also take three times as long as you expect, so be sure to take this into consideration when projecting cash flow for your new business idea.

Start off small. Don't try to bite off more than you can chew. When I expanded *Show Mummy the Money* into a national magazine, I did in fact bite off more than I could chew. Be sure you test your concept – and not just with your friends, as most good friends will simply cheer, 'Great! You're onto a winner!' Few will give genuine feedback. Don't be afraid to go to market where your real customers await; it's their feedback you really need.

So go and do your research now!

Appendix:

Where

you can get help

United Kingdom

Networking sites
www.britishchambers.org.uk
The British Chambers of Commerce (BCC) is the national body for a powerful and influential Network of Accredited Chambers of Commerce across the UK; a network that directly serves not only its member businesses but the wider business community.

The BCC is the Ultimate Business Network. No other business organisation has its geographic spread. Every Chamber sits at the very heart of its local business community providing representation, services, information and guidance to its members. The BCC works with government and leading organisations such as RBS, BT and Microsoft

www.wbda.co.uk
The Women's Business Development Agency provides specific support and advice you need to start and sustain your own business. Their website tells you all about them and the free advice and

training services that they offer both face-to-face and online.

www.homebusinessnetwork.co.uk
The Home Business Network is one of the UK's key micro and home business support organisations. This site is aimed at helping businesses to grow. Through the HBN you can link up with other business owners in your local community and throughout the UK.

Membership of this site does cost; however, the site does still provide a lot of free information through its Briefing Papers, Home Business Magazine and affiliated network links.

www.is4profit.com
Launched in 2001, this independent internet-based business offers information and advice for UK SME/small businesses, as well as a Small Business Directory (b2b directory)

www.horsesmouth.co.uk
Horsesmouth is the social network for informal mentoring - you can search for a mentor, be a mentor, or just browse the inspirational profiles and stories on the site. Click on the "Spotlight on Business" It's safe, it's free and it's facilitated by the Department for Business, Innovation and Skills (BIS) - see later section on 'Inventions'.

www.theathenanetwork.com
The Athena Network serves women in business by raising their profile, contributing to the achievement of their goals and by providing exposure to a diverse range of business success models. This is another means to network yourself with like-minded women passionate about growing and developing their business. Athena Network provides numerous trainings and workshops, some designed to help those new to networking, others catering for more experienced networkers.

www.businesseventscalendar.co.uk
You can find out about business networking events, seminars, training etc in regions across the UK. You can register your company events, and for regular e-mail updates on here for free, too.

www.fsb.org.uk

The Federation of Small Businesses is the UK's largest campaigning pressure group promoting and protecting the interests of the self-employed and owners of small firms. Formed in 1974, it now has 215,000 members across 33 regions and 230 branches. They can line you up with Financial and Business Services provided by partnerships with market-leading corporate organisations. The FSB also lobbies government with direct access to politicians and civil servants in the UK and European Parliaments. Membership fees are based on number of employees.

Government sites

The UK government supports small business and there are a number of organisations that can provide business owners with assistance and advice.

www.businesslink.gov.uk

This is a really great site set up by the UK government, designed purely to help provide advice and guidance to businesses both established and those in the start-up phase. Full of advice on a vast range of business topics and links to other information sources, it's a fantastic site to visit for direction and, best of all, it's free.

It helps your business save time and money by giving you instant access to clear, simple, and trustworthy information. It is developed in partnership with subject experts within government and relevant business-support organisations to help you comply with regulations and improve your performance. Whether you're starting up, already running a business, or looking to grow and develop, they can help you. Want to know about IT and e-Commerce? That's on the site too!

www.companieshouse.gov.uk

The official UK government register of UK companies. They incorporate and dissolve limited companies. They also examine and store company information delivered under the Companies Act and related legislation.

www.hmrc.gov.uk

HM Revenue & Customs (HMRC) was formed in 2005, following

the merger of Inland Revenue and HM Customs and Excise Departments. Their website provides information and services related to taxes and specific social policy services. It's a good starting point for finding out about your tax obligations and entitlements as a business owner. The website also provides access to interactive calculators and tools for a range of activities, including personal tax summaries, PAYE, National Insurance, VAT and Corporation Tax.

www.uktradeinvest.gov.uk

UK Trade & Investment (UKTI) works to provide business opportunities, expert trade advice and support to UK-based companies wishing to grow their business overseas.

www.supply2.gov.uk

Log in or register now to access public sector contract opportunities which could provide your company with a new route to business growth. The free Online Search now allows all suppliers to access full details of lower-value contract information - nationwide.

Supply2.gov.uk also provides notification of lower-value contract alerts in a local location of your choice - free of charge.

www.food.gov.uk

The Food Standards Agency is an independent Government department set up by an Act of Parliament in 2000 to protect the public's health and consumer interests in relation to food. Their vision: "Safe food and healthy eating for all". If you are thinking of setting up a business related to food in any way, they can help advise regarding legislation, food safety and hygiene, including HACCP (Hazard Analysis and Critical Control Points), nutrition and labelling. They have regional links and can often be contacted via your local city councils too. See the section on Birmingham City Council who have a link to source the FSA's free guide on how to comply with food law

www.netregs.gov.uk

NetRegs provides free environmental guidance for small and medium-sized businesses in the UK. They help you to understand what you need to do to comply with environmental law and protect the environment and may even help you to save money by showing you ways to use your resources more efficiently.

www.direct.gov.uk

Want to get contact details of your local councils, or those in the regions where you want to do business? Check out the A to Z on this site which lists county councils, borough and district councils and unitary authorities throughout England, Northern Ireland, Scotland and Wales.

Funding

The Government sites listed earlier have funding and grants information galore, but here are some others worth browsing:

www.businesslink.gov.uk/bdotg/action

Link to the Small Firms Loan Guarantee, a joint venture between the BERR (Dept. for Business, Enterprise and Regulatory Reform) and participating approved lenders.

www.bbaa.org.uk

If you are looking for an alternative source of funding you may wish to consider using the British Business Angels Association. A business angel is an investor or affluent individual who provides development capital or seed funding for a business start-up. Quite often business angels are retired and are prepared to invest their business skills as well as capital into new and developing enterprises.

www.bvca.co.uk

If you need capital on a grand scale, the British Venture Capital Association might be able to help. The BVCA is the industry body and public policy advocate for the private equity and venture capital industry in the UK for the benefit of investors and entrepreneurs and is another type or form of business angel. This site also has some great articles on it, even if you don't need capital.

www.princes-trust.org.uk

The Prince's Trust is a charity which provides training, mentoring and financial assistance to help young people gain employment or to start up a business. It can provide low interest loans up to £4000, test marketing grants of £250-500 and mentoring support if you are 18-30 and unemployed.

www.kickstarter.com

A new way to fund ideas and endeavours if you have a creative idea or venture. You do need to be invited to have your project accepted, then people pledge funding.

Inventions

www.bis.gov.uk (this will replace www.berr.gov.uk & www.dius.gov.uk)

The mission of the Department for Business, Innovation and Skills is "building a dynamic and competitive UK economy by: creating the conditions for business success; promoting innovation, enterprise and science; and giving everyone the skills and opportunities to succeed".

What they do: Enterprise and Business support.

They comprise 4 Executive agencies: Company House, Insolvency Service, Intellectual Property Office and National Measurement Office.

They have over 100 Delivery partners, including 25 Sector Skills Councils, 9 Reciprocal Development Agencies and 7 Research Councils.

www.ipo.gov.uk

The Intellectual Property Office can help you get the right type of protection for your creation or invention.

www.nesta.org.uk

NESTA is the National Endowment for Science, Technology and the Arts - a unique body with a mission to make the UK more innovative. They invest in early-stage companies, inform and shape policy, and deliver practical programmes that inspire others to solve the big challenges of the future.

www.innovate-design.co.uk
Innovate is a group of award-winning product designers that specialise in turning ideas and inventions into viable, marketable products. They offer support and advice through the whole invention process: how to patent an idea, advice on product patents and product design development to sell the idea to industry.

www.own-it.org
Own-It provides intellectual property advice for creative businesses. Membership is free and members can attend events, access event podcasts, templates of legal contracts, legal advice and book one-to-one IP advice sessions with lawyers.

www.lda.designingdemand.org.uk
Through the Design Council, this business support programme helps businesses become more competitive, by guiding managers to spot design opportunities and assist them with design projects. It's part of the Solutions for Business package of business support products, government-backed and publicly funded.

www.inventionsuk.com
With almost 15 years experience in transforming product ideas into global market realities, it offers confidential advice on the commercialisation of intellectual property (IP) on a fee-for-service plus % of proceeds basis.

Other

www.inlandrevenue.org.uk
This site provides information on a variety of tax-related topics, whether from a UK perspective, or as they are handled in a host of other countries, if you search on their sponsored links and related search engine.

www.start.biz

Since 1984 the National Business Register has provided free information advice and support to make it easy to set up a new business, new company, trade mark or brand and domain name. To register a business name you need to check that someone else hasn't already taken it! A good start is to visit the NBR's online name search. They also provide a comprehensive service related to company and domain name registration for which there are various charges.

www.thebestof.co.uk/national/uk/business-guide/businessnetworking-organisations

Find the best Business/Networking Organisations in UK as recommended by local UK people in the best of UK's Business/Networking Organisations directory.

www.smallbusiness.co.uk

This site provides general information on starting and operating a small or home-based business. As this is its only area of focus, it's particularly useful, whereas some of the other sites listed cater for both small and large business. It's an online service only, though, so they don't offer individual business advice by phone or email.

www.prowess.org.uk

An association of organisations and individual entrepreneurs, Prowess promotes business ownership by women. Development news, success stories, sharing of best practice, quality standards and a variety of publications can all be accessed via this link.

www.businessdirectory-uk.com

You can register as a member to have your business listed on this site for a fee, paid through PayPal. You will get a lifetime listing with a link to your website, as well as links to various other sites and networks offering business advice.

www.businessgalore.co.uk

Founded in June 2008, Business Galore was set up as a free

directory to help you find online businesses in the UK. You can list your business there too.

www.ehow.com
How to do just about everything!

www.resultscorporation.co.uk
Click on to their free marketing newsletter or read some of the articles and case studies to help you get some ideas for better marketing results.

www.themarketingcoach.co.uk
Another site that could help you develop your marketing strategy.

www.smallbizpod.co.uk
Look no further for some inspiring podcast interviews with entrepreneurs, or practical advice for small businesses and start-ups.

www.all4kidsuk.com
This site is fantastic to see just what businesses are out there catering for anything to do with babies and kids – have a browse for some inspirational ideas, and maybe some vital contacts, once you have decided just what your venture might be.

www.fashionunited.co.uk
Want to join a business-to-business (b2b) platform revolving around the fashion industry with networking and updates worldwide? Then this might be for you. If you are thinking of venturing into the fashion arena, then it might give some insights into trends and future opportunities.

www.mumsclub.co.uk
Mums Club provides everything you need to make your dream of being in business a reality. Right here is where mums meet, network and discuss the daily business versus family issues.

By Region
London
www.businesslink.gov.uk/london
Part of the Government site Business Link, but tailored for businesses in the London region. Like the other Business Link sites, it's full of information covering taxes, employment, growing your business, buying and selling a business, to name but a few of the topics.

www.london.gov.uk/gla
On the Greater London Authority website, have a look at the FAQs (Frequently Asked Questions) about Economic Development, and follow the link to the London Development Agency.

www.lda.gov.uk
The London Development Agency site is ideal if you want to know more about the support available for start-up businesses, especially Small and Medium Enterprises (SMEs) in the London area.. Look here for pointers on funding, science and technology and innovation.

www.ltnetwork.org
The London Technology Network, part of Enterprise Europe Network, is a not-for-profit organisation aimed at helping knowledge transfer between science and technology research institutions and business, to foster innovation and competitiveness. They can find suitable consultants, promote partnerships between business and research, and have links with more than 500 European technology support groups in 40 countries.

www.millipod.com
Millipod reaches 500 small-biz entrepreneurs by weekly e-newsletter. Their networking events are held throughout the year in Kent and London. They help with marketing, PR, IT, training, sales, websites – with sound business advice. Being a small independent company themselves they understand the challenges you face.

www.london-crossriverpartnership.org
Grants and loans for new and small businesses in London South Central.

England, South-East
www.seeda.co.uk
As Regional Development Agency for the South-East, SEEDA has one aim - to support the economic development of the region. Working at local, regional, national and international levels to attract inward investment, help businesses reach their full potential and win practical support from a range of partners. They bring funding into the region to help the economic growth of the South East.

www.ekentwib.org.uk
East Kent Women in Business is a branch of the Women in Business organisation open to any business woman who feels that by talking with other women from a variety of business backgrounds, she can benefit her own development as well as her business.

England, South-West
www.southwestrda.org.uk
The official Regional Development Agency for the South-West, working in key areas such as: social, economic and physical regeneration of local communities; inward investment; business development and support.

England, North-East
www.businesslink.gov.uk/northeast
Business & Enterprise North East delivers the Business Link service across the whole of the North East to provide the region's businesses and those who wish to start-up in business with support that is credible, efficient, targeted and focussed.

www.sunderlandbusinessnetwork.co.uk
Link up with this network comprising 8 business clubs and over 800 business in the Sunderland region. Independent advice and peer

support, with briefings and meetings. Membership fees are based on number of employees, with a discount if you are in your first year of trading.

England, North-West
www.businesslink.gov.uk/northwest
Business Link is an easy-to-use business support, advice and information service funded by government and managed in the North West by the Northwest Regional Development Agency.

www.nwda.co.uk
The official Regional Development Agency for the North-West, managing the economic development and regeneration of the region; promoting business efficiency, inward investment and competitiveness for a stronger economy.

www.business-network-north.co.uk
A regional networking site linked to Business Network UK. Events, news stories and members forum for the North. See the site for corporate and individual membership fees, terms and condition.

England, Midlands
www.businesslink.gov.uk/westmidlands
The BusinessLink for this region, covering start up support and business development, newsletters and case studies, to name but a few of the resources available.

www.emda.org.uk and www.advantagewm.co.uk
The East Midlands Development Agency and Advantage West Midlands are the development agencies responsible for providing advice and support for businesses in the Midlands. News about local business success stories, case studies, funding opportunities and much more!

www.birmingham.gov.uk
Have a look at the website for Birmingham City Council and search

under "Small Business". You'll find a directory of organisations that can help, advice on how to get funding, information on how to do business with the Council and even a free guide from the Food Standards Agency called "Safer Food, Better Business"

The Council manages a Loans to Small to Medium Sized Enterprises (SMEs) Programme which is delivered by Aston Reinvestment Trust (ART) and Advantage West Midlands. This will provide loans of between £10,000 and £50,000 to entrepreneurs looking to create sustainable new businesses; and existing businesses, including social enterprises, in Birmingham.

www.wmictcluster.org

The West Midlands ICT Cluster is a great site for finding links to other support organisations, whether for news about regional initiatives, the benefits of relocating to the Midlands, business or financial support, research and development, or even information about international trade.

www.bestforbusiness.com and www.blclub.co.uk

Created by the staff at Business Insight, Central Library, Birmingham, Best for Business provides free business information covering all topics, with a slight West Midlands bias for more specific services such as grants and tenders. There are over 500 fact sheets on the site under the Business Advice heading as well as Know How guides.

Scotland

Official Scottish Government statistics show that Small and Medium-sized Enterprises (SMEs) now account for 99% of all Scottish businesses and for over half of all private sector employment – underlining the pivotal role of small firms in our economy and communities.

www.scotland.gov.uk

As part of its aim to foster long term sustainable economic growth in Scotland the devolved Scottish Government has a range of initiatives to encourage business start-ups and grow existing businesses. Support grants are made up of Investment Grants - the

Regional Selective Assistance (RSA) is the main national scheme of financial assistance to industry and Innovation Grants - a range of funding to assist the research and development of innovative products and processes. These also include the SMART:SCOTLAND scheme and the SEEKIT programme.

www.bgateway.com and www.hiebusiness.co.uk
Part of BusinessLink, Business Gateway is the site for new and growing businesses in Scotland, with the second site aimed at the Highlands and Islands.

www.scottishbusinessgrants.gov.uk
Scottish Enterprise can provide financial assistance to new and existing businesses in Scotland through its innovation (SMART: SCOTLAND) and investment (RSA) grants.

www.scottishbusinessblog.co.uk
You can subscribe to the newsletter on this blog which helps network businesses across Scotland. And just click on their map and that will put you in touch with events and networking companies in that area.

www.thriveforbusiness.co.uk
Thrive is a series of networking clubs in the Edinburgh and Glasgow areas. Have a look at the site – bringing together people from small and medium enterprise companies (SMEs). Business-to-business (b2b) support and advice, with an initial try-before-you-buy fee available. You do have to commit to one year's membership and your company does have to be represented at club meetings.

www.envirowise.gov.uk/scotland
This regional arm of Envirowise aims through its Small Business Support Programme to provide free assistance to Scotland's small business community in order to realise cost savings, new sales, reduced risk and competitive advantage through improvements in resource efficiency.

Wales

www.business-support-wales.gov.uk

Flexible Support for Business – a part of the Government site Business Link, but targeted at businesses in Wales. You might be interested to find out more about their Inclusion Challenge Fund which offers additional support to people from under-represented groups, or their Single Investment Fund - Local, which is a capital fund for small to medium-sized businesses (SMEs). This fund offers financial support between £1,000-£5,000, covering up to 40% of eligible costs.

www.wales.gov.uk

The Welsh Assembly is the devolved government of Wales. On their site click on the tab for funding and you'll find out more about their funding and grants options. They can tailor advice to your needs, helping to develop a funding package enabling you to start up, expand, modernise, restructure, or to develop new products or processes.

www.bcnpt.co.uk

Business Connect Neath Port Talbot Ltd is a private, limited non-profit making organisation offering expert advice and training on a huge range of business topics. For individuals considering self-employment general services are free, while for established businesses in Wales they provide a wide range of free and subsidised professional services comprising advice, support and practical help with issues such as: raising funding (grants & loans); writing business plans; cash-flow; accounts; marketing; finding contracts; websites and search engine optimisation.

www.biznetwales.co.uk

Find out more about how to join one or more of the 6 Welsh Business Networks, what membership costs and what they offer.

www.walesonline.co.uk

A great site for updates on Welsh news, including what's happening on the business front, stories, articles and blogs, as well as links to digital copies of *Business in Wales* magazine and other publications.

www.venturewales.com
Venture Wales is a leading business support organisation in Wales, the "first choice for all small and medium sized companies and entrepreneurs looking for advice and support on any aspect of their business". They are a deliverer of the Welsh Assembly Government's General Support for Business pre- and post-start programmes and have partnership or links with other groups such as Inland Revenue, International Business Wales, and Finance Wales

Northern Ireland
www.nibusinessinfo.co.uk
Practical online advice for Northern Ireland business from the Government-driven Business Link and provided by Invest Northern Ireland. Includes downloadable forms to use when dealing with government departments and agencies, as well as interactive tools to help you run your business.

www.enterpriseni.com
Enterprise Northern Ireland (ENI) is the organisation representing the network of Local Enterprise Agencies in Northern Ireland. Local Enterprise Agencies (LEAs) are independent, locally based not-for-profit companies set up to support small business development and to undertake economic development activity.

www.northernireland.gov.uk
Check out the site for the Northern Ireland Executive, part of the devolved government, the Northern Ireland Assembly. Their A to Z tab will give you all the links to relevant government departments as well as the sites of all the Borough Councils you might need.

www.belfastcity.gov.uk
Get onto this local government site and hook into the Belfast Entrepreneurs Network

www.derrycity.gov.uk
And why not try this one for Derry, too!

www.borderpeople.info

Provided by the North/South Ministerial Council, the Border People website is the central access point for cross-border mobility information on the island of Ireland. There are a variety of links for business start-up support, including several of those detailed in this Appendix.

Index

market trend 16

D

dance instructor 112
D'arcy Brown 7
database management 125
Days to Amaze 37
De Montparnasse, Kiki 40
DeHart, Jacob 51
Department for Business, Innovation and
  Skills 210
depilatory cream 9
design competitions
  business designs 122
  T-shirts 51
desktop publishing 62
'dessert bar' restaurants 32
detergents, high-end 39
Didyourememberthemilk.com 106
Dietrich, Stephen 91
differentiating, products and services 16
digital cameras, training for use 143
direct mail newsletter 123
direct selling
  benefits 106
  consultant to the consultants 116
distribution channel, choosing 181
DIY furniture and accessories 98
dog biscuits, homemade 92
dog food
  gourmet treats 92
  recipes 69
dog trainer 128
dogs
  clothing and accessories 143
  day care 152
Doherty, Fraser 154
dolls clothes
  Baby Born wardrobe 42
  particular doll models 117
domain names & extensions,
  registering 193
domestic help 22
DoMyStuff.com 23
doula 123
Dream Dinners meal assembly concept
  94
dried herbs and spices 81
Driving Miss Daisy cab service 27
drop shipment 136
drop-off stores, eBay 41
duvet covers, handcrafted, designer 79
DVD burner 156
Dyson, James 10
Dyson vacuum cleaners 10

E

eating on the run 32
eBay
  getting market value 147
  pick-up service 138
ebooks, writing and selling 118
eHow 55, 213
Ecolimo limousine service 21
Edible Blooms 137
Elance freelancer website 121
electrolyte replacement tablets 30
email addresses 195
E-marketing 199
employee relationship consultant 112
employment agencies, mature
  workers 26
England websites
  Midlands 216
  North-East 215
  North-West 216
  South-East 215
  South-West 215
entrepreneurs, successful 2
environmental guidance, NetRegs 208
environmentally friendly
  consumption 19
EnviroShopperTM shopping bags 21
Eons business website 27
erotic adult products 40
errand runner 144
Etsy handmade goods 34
events co-ordinator 63
Evlove Intimates lingerie 18
exotic birds, breeding 90
expense reduction service 141
extreme makeover classes 95

F

fads 16
Fairy Cake Mother, The 81
family day care carer 117
Feuerwear bags and belts 36
financial analysis 189
fish, breeding 89
fitness
  business opportunities 28
  facilities for obese children 29
  freelance gym instructor 153
  personal instructor 110
flower arrangements, wedding 136
flower bulbs, selling 148
Flujo office furniture and accessories 40
Flylite luggage service 24
food

Also published by Accent Press

Don't Feed The Ducks!

Liam O'Connell

Don't just feed the ducks and wait for something to happen. Do something about it now!

Through a series of real life stories, observations and innovative ideas, Liam O'Connell explains how anybody can create an extraordinary successful business.
Liam believes in harnessing the power of passionate people to create real life business results. His innovative and off-the-wall style is equally entertaining and thought-provoking. Liam has the ability to communicate positively and his enthusiasm is absolutely contagious.

ISBN 9781907016523
£10.99

My Fire's Gone Out!

Liam O'Connell

A contemporary motivational book – the new "Who Moved My Cheese!"

My Fire's Gone Out! is a simple, funny and yet profound story about coping with change.
The fire is a metaphor for what is really important to you in your life or your work.
In this fast-paced modern world we live in,we are faced with many challenges and complex choices. Sometimes our personal fire can go out and this book can help you get that spark back to relight your fire!
Read it in an hour and change your life for good!

ISBN 9781907016516
£5.99